Meet the Authors

Dr. Maria C. Guilott "Margo" has been an educator for 40 years. She received a Master's Degree and a Ph.D. from Tulane University and has been a classroom teacher from second grade to the college level, a high school administrator, a district supervisor, assistant superintendent for curriculum and instruction and, most recently, an assistant professor in Educational Leadership at The University of Southern Mississippi. She spent 36 years in the K-12 world, was the author of multiple programs designed to serve at-risk learners, supervised instruction, conducted professional development, guided curriculum development, strategic planning, and principal supervision. In a district of 35,000 students, she committed to writing curriculum using *Understanding by Design* as the framework, making it available on-line. It was the implementation of the curriculum that prompted her to pursue the collegial learning walks as a viable process for principals to use. Through her work with the Instructional Leadership Center at The University of Southern Mississippi and her work with Authentic Education, she and her colleagues developed the process now called the Collegial Learning Walks.

Dr. Gaylynn Parker, a former professor in the Department of Educational Leadership and School Counseling at The University of Southern Mississippi, is a staunch believer that our work in the field of education should be about continuous improvement and lifelong learning for all involved. During the past thirty-one years, Dr. Parker has served as a teacher, lead teacher, media specialist, curriculum and instruction specialist and instructional consultant. In each position, she has taken leadership roles in mentoring new teachers, preparing and delivering professional development, and facilitating numerous team meetings. In addition, she has worked diligently to improve classroom instruction by ensuring that a rigorous guaranteed and viable curriculum was in place through the coordination of teacher workshops and job-embedded coaching, and/or follow-up for developing and revising PreK – Grade 12 language arts and social studies units. As a National Board Certified teacher, she mentored other candidates who pursued the process. She was a district facilitator for Quality School teams and served as a Media Specialist. Nationally, she served as a member of Academy XVI for the National Staff Development Council and serves on the Board of Directors for the Mississippi Staff Development Council. Also, she taught computer, literature, and writing courses for Mississippi Gulf Coast Community College and Tulane University. Through her work with the Instructional Leadership Center, she was instrumental in working to make the Collegial Learning Walks a value added component for any school district with any demographic circumstances.

Acknowledgements

While we know that students acquire knowledge on a daily basis, our mission has been to encourage the tasks that enable students to make meaning of that knowledge, then be able to transfer what they have learned to greater depths of knowledge and to other situations, that is, to true understanding. In order to reach that goal, we have developed a protocol to bring administrators and teachers into conversations in order to *know* when students are reaching transfer. The walks are generative in nature, yet prescriptive in the sense that they are invaluable in ensuring increased student achievement through distinct changes in teachers' classroom practices. However, we could not have achieved this feat alone.

A special thanks to all of our esteemed colleagues, practicing administrators in the field, and teachers who have taken the risk to prove that viable options do exist to promote increased professional development for teachers that results in increased learning for our nation's most valuable resource: our children. Through our research with members of the Instructional Leadership Center, a member of the International Network of Principal Centers, directed by Dr. Ronald A. Styron, and through promoting the work of Grant Wiggins and Jay McTighe, *Understanding by Design* and *Schooling by Design*, we have been able to develop a method of Collegial Learning Walks that supports structured dialogue about learning from the *learner's* perspective.

In fact, the idea for the book was born through a conversation with Leslie Collings, a principal in Rocky View School District in Canada. She told us we needed to write a "little book," a how-to-book about Collegial Learning Walks—a booklet so crucial that "if the school were on fire, we'd rush back inside to get it." That was the impetus for *A Value-Added Decision*.

Kim Brandon, principal of Northeast Middle School in St. Louis, Missouri, is another person, to whom, like Leslie, we owe a tremendous amount of gratitude for encouraging us and contributing to our research.

Given that the intended audience is principals and assistant school administrators, we appreciate the help we received from Dr. Ronald Styron and Dr. Grant Wiggins who gave us feedback based on the research and professional perspectives. However, since the process discussed in the book supports the work of teachers, we believe it will also appeal to teacher leaders, professional developers, and district office staff who recognize the role the principal plays in teachers' professional development. In other words, the book is for practitioners interested in helping teachers transfer their learning into their practices. A special thanks to Carol Young who read the book from a teacher's perspective and offered suggestions for improvement.

Furthermore, the many iterations of the process evolved while working with principals across the nation (and in Canada and Japan), have contributed to making the contents of this book grounded in the day-to-day practices of actual schools. The intention is to engage the teachers and to turn ordinary schools into extraordinary learning environments where teachers share common understandings and are constantly seeking collegial and collaborative growth. Again, special thanks are sent to our many colleagues, too numerous to list, who have worked to promote student learning through the development of our Collegial Learning Walks.

A Value Added Decision

To Support the Delivery of High Level Instruction

MARIA C. GUILOTT AND GAYLYNN PARKER

outskirtspress
DENVER, COLORADO

The opinions expressed in this manuscript are solely the opinions of the author and do not represent the opinions or thoughts of the publisher. The author has represented and warranted full ownership and/or legal right to publish all the materials in this book.

A Value Added Decision
To Support the Delivery of High Level Instruction
All Rights Reserved.
Copyright © 2012 Maria C. Guilott and Gaylynn Parker
v4.0 r1.0

Cover Photo © 2012 JupiterImages Corporation. All rights reserved - used with permission.

This book may not be reproduced, transmitted, or stored in whole or in part by any means, including graphic, electronic, or mechanical without the express written consent of the publisher except in the case of brief quotations embodied in critical articles and reviews.

Outskirts Press, Inc.
http://www.outskirtspress.com

ISBN: 978-1-4327-8576-5

Outskirts Press and the "OP" logo are trademarks belonging to Outskirts Press, Inc.

PRINTED IN THE UNITED STATES OF AMERICA

Preface

The essence of this book involves the process resulting from the work of practitioners refining and perfecting a way to increase teacher efficacy and self-reflection. Many thoughtful educators have vetted the process and have contributed to its dynamic and generative effect. Administrators from across the country, Canada and Japan have tried the process and offered suggestions to improve it. Teachers who have experienced the process have also added their suggestions for ways to implement it with minimum resistance. When implemented with fidelity and intentionality, the process is a gift for professional growth for everyone involved, and, most importantly, it is designed to promote increased student achievement. As teacher developers, we believe we must follow the "Release of Responsibility" model (I do, you watch; I do, you help; you do, I help; you do, I watch), as a general schema for the development of transfer ability at any age, in any domain. In other words, as facilitators of teacher learning, we must also follow this schema if we expect teachers to transfer what they learned in a classroom or in a workshop into their own classrooms. To adhere to the "Release of Responsibility," we are recommending Collegial Learning Walks as a value-added decision to help teachers actually apply their collective learning to engage students in meaning-making leading to transfer.

Table of Contents

INTRODUCTION 1

CHAPTER 1   Overview of Established Process 11
Provides a background of the process and outlines the questions to be addressed

CHAPTER 2   How is the intention for the outcome critical to the process? 17
Provides the non-negotiable aspects of the process

CHAPTER 3   The Boomerang Strategies 33
Discusses a process that goes hand-in-hand with Collegial Learning Walks and helps the principal set the rationale

CHAPTER 4   What are the mechanics of the process? 45
Provides the actual agreements, protocols, and questions to be used in the entire process

CHAPTER 5   How is every member of the Collegial Learning Walk a learner? 69
Provides the thinking behind everyone, including the principal, being a learner as described by a practitioner

CHAPTER 6	What are some of the possible steps in the implementation process?........77 Offers suggestions on how to implement the process in the school
CHAPTER 7	How is the process synergy in action?...81 Provides an example of how synergy is created by the process itself
CHAPTER 8	How is the process a continuous growth model? ....89 Points to the professional growth opportunities that emerge as long as the process remains non-evaluative
CHAPTER 9	How does the process build a learning community?.......................93 Provides concrete examples of meaningful and practical collaboration that result from the implementation of the process
CHAPTER 10	What is the "magic" of the process? How does it work best? ....97 Provides the teacher perspective from those who have experienced the Collegial Learning Walks
CHAPTER 11	What are the "do nots" to be avoided at all cost? ....103 Provides specifics to avoid in order to ensure success

CHAPTER 12   Conclusion 107
              Pulls together the concepts discussed in the
              text

APPENDIX A   Collegial Learning Walks
              Summary... 109
              This attachment contains a summary of
              the Collegial Learning Walks Process

APPENDIX B   Practitioners cited in the text......... 115
              This attachment contains contact information for practitioners whose comments are cited in the text

REFERENCES 119

Introduction

Through our collective seventy-one years of experience in our noble profession, we have searched and researched for ways to make reflective practice a standard commitment. As classroom teachers we continually asked ourselves, "Would we have wanted our own children in this classroom today? Did we do everything that we could do to reach every student?" Our answers were often full of doubt. Later, as we became administrators, we continued trying to find ways to help teachers make learning come alive for *all* students. Then, we realized, **WE DO HAVE THE ANSWERS**! Using a variation of the cognitive coaching process promoted by Art Costa and Bob Garmston and a well orchestrated reflective process that has undergone numerous iterations, our Collegial Learning Walks (CLWs) are now thoroughly and qualitatively research-based and ready to help change the culture of instructional practice for any school or district.

At this point, this book is primarily for administrators seeking to help their teachers improve their reflective practice. We already have an incredible amount of research available on effective planning, strategies that work, and structures to support them all, yet we are told by administrators that there is still a "disconnect" between what administrators believe is good instruction and what teachers believe good instruction looks like in practice. Certainly, we also know that the evaluation of teachers is not something a principal can dismiss lightly. Monitoring instruction for accountability of performance and quality assurance are both essential components of a building administrator's role. Evaluation of teaching performance is currently a highly contested topic, as some states are trying to link student performance to teachers' merit pay. The fear that this idea has generated will take years to overcome. Nevertheless, the building administrator, the instructional leader and the teacher evaluator must do the right thing and must make sure that quality instruction is present in all classrooms for all children.

Teacher evaluation, cumbersome and problematic as it might be, is a key factor in maintaining quality instruction at the school level. In fact, value added measures assigned to teacher evaluation are quickly becoming a reality despite voiced objections from educators and interested community members. The pursuit for distinguishing "good" teachers from "bad" teachers has captured the attention of a politically charged climate causing a veritable tsunami of accountability data to inundate an already saturated field. A plethora of questions emerge when we consider the ramifications of such a "logical strategy" in school reform. Some of the more obvious ones are the following: How will the non-core subject teachers be evaluated? What about all the factors that affect student performance not related to teacher performance? However, we are neither defending nor attacking the concept. Unfortunately, effectively evaluating teacher performance is a task that administrators have skirted, or completely euphemized, to avoid having the courageous conversations necessary to let teachers know when their performance is marginal at best. Sadly, we have accepted mediocrity as the norm.

Principals as instructional leaders, not just as building

INTRODUCTION

managers, must remain prominent in the decision-making arena. Therefore, as such, they need tools to help their teachers improve their practice. The Collegial Learning Walks described represent a powerful tool that is time efficient and effective. If building administrators have to accept and work with the concept of value added as a part of teacher evaluation, they will also need a way to develop instructional effectiveness with their faculty and quickly build a culture that promotes engagement in professional dialogue on a regular basis. In actuality, this is precisely the intended outcome of Collegial Learning Walks.

We do know that attending to knowledge, skills, and attitude is essential in the professional development of each faculty member. However, some may say that attitude is the hardest to change because it is not something that can be put on a Power Point or gained by participating in a workshop or by reading a book. The Collegial Learning Walks promote the professional culture, by design and in practice, and address attitude in a powerful and indirect way. Participants feel empowered and supported as they examine learning through real learning communities where everyone's voice counts and no one's ideas are discounted. Since these are not one shot efforts, participating teachers continue to grow intellectually, using each moment as a brand new learning opportunity that results in increased student achievement.

As has been our practice, we also know that teachers are hired based upon their ability to complete an approved certifying program of studies at the university level and on their ability to pass a professional exam. In other words, teachers have to meet the entry-level requirements of their profession. Other criteria for hiring are locally determined, or decided by an expressed need. Once in the system, teachers comply with district requirements to earn the cherished tenure, a double-edged sword that has rewarded excellent teachers and protected apathetic, unengaged teachers. Acceptance of the reality we face is essential if we are going to work toward continuous improvement. We do not have to like it or agree with it. We just have to accept it and become ambitious enough to build hope into our noble profession by creating structures and practices that part from the accepted norm and include what we know works.

Beyond handing the teacher the curriculum, and perhaps a handbook, what other supports can building leaders offer brand new teachers that are not directly linked to the feared evaluation process? A mentor teacher is often assigned in hopes that the more experienced teacher will help the novice get acclimated. Beyond that, seeing learning in action as it is happening is not a typical occurrence in most public school settings. The Collegial Learning Walks work especially well with new teachers who, like sponges, want to absorb everything to help them with their own learning curve. Experienced teachers who have become jaded by past ineffective evaluation protocols see value in the collegial learning walks as well. The experienced teacher may begin with a jaundiced eye but is quickly motivated by a principal open to learning and able to facilitate the learning of others. Although it may sound like Shangri-la, the truth is that if the principal commits to the process, the learning climate improves for everyone involved.

During our tenures as educators, we have lived through several reform movements that met with minimal success. Spanning from the 1955 catalyst *Johnny Can't Read* to the current *Race to the Top* federal initiative, well-meaning

INTRODUCTION

efforts have, in many cases, merely caused teachers to become cynical and left them wondering if "this too shall pass." As teacher unionization crystallized across the nation, teacher resistance escalated almost to the point of militancy, polarizing discourse and building resentment for both administrators and teachers. Through extensive research, we then created standards of best practice, curriculum standards, and a myriad of evaluation and/or supervision tools to provide feedback and support for teachers and for student learning. Thus, why have we failed to achieve intense cultures of instructional practice based upon continuous improvement in student learning?

We have tried to compensate for our shortcomings in public education by placing blame wherever possible. Are the universities not adequately preparing young people as they enter the profession? Are our induction processes flawed? Do we not have enough teachers or are we not paying them competitive salaries? Is student discipline practically nonexistent? Are the parents not involved in their children's education? Do principals not know how to be instructional leaders? Are many teachers isolated? Do we not have enough time? Does the curriculum need revamping? Are the high stakes tests used to audit performance unreasonable? Are local school boards not hiring the right people? Has the authority of teachers and schools been completely eroded? Answers to all of these questions hold a piece of the puzzle, but the full answer is one that we do have and can readily access if we put our minds to it. We have great evaluation tools, snapshots that can be captured electronically and scored immediately, as well as observation protocols. **What we do not have is a way to use our collective thinking to generate mental models that develop common understandings of the learning process through**

non-evaluative techniques and that promote teacher reflection on depths of student understanding of the content being presented—a main purpose of our Collegial Learning Walks.

Understandably, with the current state of education, public expectations and concerns are at an all time high. Teachers are already feeling the intense scrutiny of being ranked against their peers relative to state testing mandates. Many of them just shut their doors and say, "Leave me alone, and let me teach!" (Reeves, 2001). This attitude causes the definition of curriculum to be revised to "what happens between the students and the teacher once the door is closed." Of course, we know that isolation is the enemy of improvement (Schmoker, 2006). In fact, separation guarantees a very personalized practice instead of a well-conceived collegial learning environment. A visible example of this self-imposed isolation is the practice of covering the window on the door to "avoid student distraction." Whether articulated or not, the message teachers send to all "intruders" is clear: "stay out." To reverse that tension, administrators, coaches, support personnel, and teachers need to share a common ground of understanding and trust. The process of Collegial Learning Walks begins by helping teachers open their classrooms to replication of best practices. As Deborah McCollum, principal of Covington High School in St. Tammany, Louisiana so aptly argues, "To engage students in learning, we have to engage the teachers first. Teachers do not want to bore their students. They want to engage them in making meaning that leads to transfer, but they do not know how. Reading about, hearing about, or talking about moving students to transfer does not automatically translate into improved classroom practice. They need to see it in action with students in their own school, not through actors

INTRODUCTION

on film or orchestrated situations. They have to experience it themselves. If they do not know what it looks like, they will not be able to design engaging lessons that lead to students' transfer of knowledge. This is particularly true if they are teaching the way they themselves were taught."

Besides the fact that teaching involves so many variables, the process itself cannot be scripted for every student. The "aha" moments of learning are the precious gems that we as teachers treasure forever. Engaging a student from acquisition to making meaning leading to transfer is what all teachers want. The problem is when teachers' efforts fail, particularly if these efforts are accompanied by detailed and approved lesson plans. What went wrong? Was it the climate for learning, the classroom management itself, the routines and procedures, the sequencing, the delivery or the assessments? Or, was it a combination of all of the aforementioned? The layers of possibilities make sorting the answers an even more daunting task when students perform as if they have never been exposed to a set of skills. When coupled with the difficulty of the learning task itself, the frustration level escalates. Mike Schmoker adds clarity to the situation by asserting that the problem is not socio-economic or a lack of funding. The number one factor contributing to student achievement is the level of instruction by the teacher in the classroom (Schmoker, 2006).

Furthermore, educational critics remind us that, as building administrators, we know that huge discrepancies exist in the levels of instruction from one side of the hall to the other. We also know that pockets of excellence occur in our buildings and everyone, including the students, knows where they are. Yet, we still tend to be satisfied with "good enough" to avoid conflict and to maintain peace. The questions we need to ask ourselves are the following: "Is mediocrity fair to the students? Do students deserve the best we have to offer? So whose children are assigned to the mediocre or poor teachers? Would we want *our* children taught by the teacher that everyone knows is marginal?" No. We would not, and we would expect the school leader to help that teacher improve or begin the dismissal process.

However, except for our master teachers who are self-motivated, the majority of teachers need and expect support and guidance. Our master teachers are the "speedboats" who quickly embrace any change initiative and successfully implement it in their classrooms. Then, we have the "barges" or the majority of teachers who move slowly but carry the bulk of the load. Sometimes the "speedboats" have to become "tugboats" for the "barges" to help them avoid the rocks that can effectively sabotage every change initiative designed to increase student achievement. We need to learn from the "speedboats," the natural learning leaders in our buildings, as change literature confirms that sustainability is the greatest challenge. We know that change is permanent when the catalyst for change is no longer there, yet the change endures because the people in the building have internalized the change. Whether a "speedboat," "barge," or "tugboat," it is our belief that all teachers want their students to learn, and it is our responsibility to facilitate that process.

Our efforts to monitor, supervise and sustain instruction have always been hampered by the complexity of the undertaking itself. Yet, we know that true accountability lies in the task(s) the student is asked to do (City, Elmore, Fiarman, & Teitel, 2009). Thus, as building administrators, how do we generate a culture of instructional practice that is synergistic, builds on everyone's expertise and honors the knowledge and skills of the people we already have in our buildings? How do we make the process of classroom observations actually work to develop a skill set tailored to our own students' needs? How do we take the learning walk process out of drudgery and compliance into meaningful engagement for everyone involved? This book will give insight into how to answer these questions and equip administrators with the tools they need to answer some of their questions about instructional practices.

CHAPTER 1

Overview of Established Process

"A man travels the world over in search of what he needs and returns home to find it."
—George Moore

Believe it or not, we have a process that, followed with intentionality and purity of purpose, will energize administrators to support students' and teachers' learning and will offer teachers opportunities for collegial conversations that lead to improvement in the actual delivery of their instruction. We say "believe it or not" because in our experiences working with school administrators, we know their first reactions are, "I know. I am already doing that. So, what's new?" When choosing to engage in the Collegial Learning Walks, we mediate each other's thinking toward increased student achievement. That is the power of this process! In fact, while developing the Collegial Learning Walks, we continually pondered the following questions:

> Have we been approaching reform in reverse, just looking for what is *not* working and pointing it out? What if, instead, we looked for what *is* working in the context of the classroom? What if we focused upon learning from the classroom experience, shared it with our colleagues in meaningful dialogue, and then transferred best practices to our own experience? What if we looked at learning as a process with no boundaries or

limits and created excellent models of what great instruction resembles in practice? What if we supported our teachers by having them learn from one another in a mediated professional environment, based, not upon what is wrong, but on what is *next*? If all learning requires a personal connection, why do we not use this fundamental premise in teacher development?

Therefore, our process is generative in nature, focuses on best instructional practices, encourages "next step" actions, and keeps student learning at the forefront of collaborative conversations. Grounded in theory and research, the Collegial Learning Walks concept is based upon a version of learning walks initially developed by Tony Alvarado and Elaine Fink and the research that led to the writing of *Instructional Rounds in Education* by City, Elmore, Fiarman &Teitel (2009). The Alvardo/Fink model was designed as an administrative tool to support instructional management. The Collegial Learning Walk is a professional development model for the people on the walk, ultimately the teachers. Therefore, this process is not a management tool. In fact, the title, *A Value Added Decision,* pretty well describes our process.

The primary purpose of the Collegial Learning Walks is to build capacity and collegiality among a community of collaborators. It creates a community that refrains from outside judgment and promotes self-evaluation and reflection from within. Trust must be present and, to build that trust, the leader must remain faithful to the process. Actually, the Collegial Learning Walks' process is best described as a method for learning about learning and developing academic conversations that grow into actionable steps in the classroom. Its essence is a non-directive protocol that provides valuable and meaningful feedback in the reflective process. Because of its brevity, it offers strategic opportunities for follow-up and support. An important consideration that one principal admitted is that it is never cumbersome. Another factor is that, in its short duration, it provides the members of the team an "aha" in action to take back and practice immediately. As George Miller pointed out in his 1956 Magic <u>7+/-2</u>, our short-term memories cannot hold very much in "M" space (Miller, 1956). The Collegial Learning Walk allows for acquisition, making meaning and transfer about learning within a short period of time.

"If," as Grant Wiggins and Jay McTighe say, "transfer is the long-term purpose of schooling," then what is transfer? These two experts also provide further clarification to this essential question. "Learning for understanding requires that curriculum and instruction address three different but interrelated academic goals: helping students (1) *acquire* important information and skills; (2) *make meaning* of that content, and (3) effectively *transfer* their learning to new situations both within school and beyond it" (Wiggins and McTighe, 2008).

A student can memorize a list, a passage, a set of facts. However, if asked to describe when or how s/he would use the information, the student will probably be at a loss. The problem is we often do a really good job with acquisition but fail to allow students to make their own meaning so that they can use it later, completely on their own, and know when and how to use it. In other words, be able to transfer it to a new and different context. A word of caution is in order here. We do not want to "throw the baby out with the bathwater." All three interrelated goals are essential. We just do not want to get stuck in acquisition and wonder why our students cannot transfer their learning and why they fail to do well on the transfer questions that appear on the standardized tests. One problem that emerges immediately is that, as educators (teachers and administrators), we formulate constructs on our own without vetting them with other colleagues. What we may consider making meaning is really still acquisition. We may think we understand transfer but in reality we do not. A common mistake is that people identify making meaning as transfer. During the making meaning process of learning, students relate facts and/or skills to some context that makes the information useful. It is also in the making meaning stage that students explore the various ways and situations in which the acquired knowledge can be used. In transfer, however, students know when to use, or not use, the facts and/or skills and are able to apply them to new situations or problems. Transfer is also meta-cognition; students know they know the information and discern for themselves when to use it. The Collegial Learning Walks give us an opportunity as educators to share and clarify our thinking and to calibrate ourselves as to what we consider *acquisition, making meaning, and transfer* relative to new, previously learned and common classroom practices.

We have captured the collective thinking of principals from Canada and Japan. Administrators from the states of Georgia, Louisiana, Mississippi, Missouri, New Jersey and Wisconsin have also shared their success stories from their uses of the Collegial Learning Walks. Therefore, in the chapters listed below, we address the major points that help readers understand the power of the Collegial Learning Walks.

How is the intention for the outcome critical to the process?

OVERVIEW OF ESTABLISHED PROCESS

What are the mechanics of the process?

How is every member of the Collegial Learning Walk a learner?

What are some of the possible steps in the implementation process?

How is the process synergy in action?

How is the process a continuous growth model?

How does the process build a learning community?

What is the "magic" of the process? How does it work best?

What are the "do nots" to be avoided at all cost?

CHAPTER 2

How is the intention for the outcome critical to the process?

Mistakes, obviously, show us what needs improving. Without mistakes, how would we know what we had to work on?"
—Peter McWilliams

One premise to which the Collegial Learning Walk team must adhere

In order for our learning walks to be unique, the prevailing thought *must not be* "What is wrong?" but *must be* "What is next?" The difference here is tremendous because we are not on a "fault-finding mission." The idea is that we all improve as a result of participating in the Collegial Learning Walk (CLW). No one has **THE** answer. We are all learners, and we are sharing what we know to scaffold our learning and multiply its effects in geometric proportions. Everyone on the walk must participate. No one goes on a Collegial Learning Walk under duress, as participation is always a choice that must be embraced. We are not on a mission to judge the teacher. We are on the walk to understand the learning process and to gauge our instruction accordingly. Our focus is not on the teacher. It is on the **LEARNER**. What the teacher has planned is important, but this does not matter if the execution of the plan is not working, that is, if the students are not "getting it." The old "sage on the stage" notion becomes the antithesis of what we want. What the students are learning in relation to the task(s) they are asked to complete is what we consider on our CLWs. Our mission is to determine if the students are in the acquisition, meaning-making, or the transfer stage of learning, and do they know what they are doing and why? In other words, how are the instruction and task(s) combined helping students move toward or reach true transfer of knowledge and skills?

"Telling" teachers how to get students to transfer has not yielded positive results and neither has threatening them with job action made a difference. Attitude cannot be legislated. A checklist of expected behaviors may point the teacher in the right direction, but it is certainly not going to ensure adherence, even with frequent monitoring of behavior. That is why our Collegial Learning Walks do not set any particular expectations. Participants look for evidence of making meaning and do not make any assumptions about how that should look. Observations are analyzed with the consideration that everyone can improve.

One obstacle that will need to be overcome is the belief teachers hold that if a team visits their classrooms, they are all there to judge their performance. This is not an evaluative process. It is *not* designed to be a part of evaluation. In fact, no paper is taken into the classroom. Nothing is written, and confidentiality is critical for the process to work. Since building trust is such a tenuous condition, everyone who participates in a learning walk must abide by the idea that what goes on and is discussed during the learning walk, stays on the learning walk. It is our intention to keep the focus on the principal, for Michael Fullan's research indicates that "the single most important factor in moving schools forward is that the principal is also a learner" (Fullan, 2009). Therefore, it is up to the principal to decide whether an assistant principal should lead the Collegial Learning Walk and has the same learner attitude and open-mindedness, i.e. a common mindset. An essential premise of this process, however, is that only administrators lead the walk. The reasoning for this is that the principal or seasoned assistant principal steps out of the classroom and can see "the big picture." The building administrator has developed tools and strategies to handle sensitive situations concerning observation and evaluation. Administrators can avoid letting a situation get complicated, and they know how to turn the discussion so that judgment and criticism remain outside the Collegial Learning Walk itself. They know how important it is to make sure that trust remains on solid ground. Also, teachers already expect to be evaluated by administrators. They are, consequently, much more likely to accept feedback from the administrator. In fact, feedback to the teacher will only be offered if the teacher requests it because the focus is not on the teacher teaching the lesson. The focus is on the "learning about learning" of the group that actually goes on the Collegial Learning Walk.

Factors related to the school's established curriculum are important to the Collegial Learning Walk process, especially in trying to determine when students are at the acquisition, meaning-making, or transfer levels of learning. It is necessary to establish a common mindset of what each stage looks like in practice. As Robert Marzano's research has determined, a guaranteed and viable curriculum is the single most important factor in student achievement (Marzano, 2003). When such a curriculum that allows for flexibility is in place, the likelihood of meeting with success by standard measures provided in the accountability system is much higher. However, a perfectly written curriculum quickly becomes a museum artifact if teachers have not been an integral part of the design process. Districts and departments of education have written curriculum that attempted to be "teacher friendly." The process typically had teachers design activities to support the goals and objectives. The product was proudly given to teachers in a binder. Unfortunately, despite best efforts to monitor curriculum implementation, the document soon became fossilized, gathering dust on the shelf. Any attempt at revision or revival was difficult at best, with more copies to be printed and old ones to be shredded. In short, this process quickly amounted to what Schmoker aptly calls "Curriculum Chaos," everyone doing his or her own thing (Schmoker, 2006).

With the advent of technology, the written document can now be uploaded to a special site for teacher access; however, this newer version can also become fossilized if it is not kept fresh. Teachers must have the mechanism to provide feedback based on their practice, and this feedback needs to be incorporated into the written and uploaded document on a regular basis. With such a document that allows for teacher discretion yet expects teacher buy-in, school building administrators are better able to support its implementation. Again, the intention for the outcome has to remain pure, beginning with the written curriculum. Although districts and experts can provide protocols and models for delivery of instruction in the written curriculum, the ultimate decisions must rest with the teacher who knows the students and what they need. The plan must "live" inside the teacher's head and move students into deeper depths of learning. Of course, this presupposes that careful planning is involved, and that the teachers have a clear understanding of the knowledge and skills students bring to the table. Without this, the plan is just a broad brush-over and a feeble attempt to "cover" the content.

Again, how the curriculum is written matters if the outcome sought is transfer of learning. *Understanding by Design* is a curriculum framework that aims at learning for making meaning and transfer. Since, according to Grant Wiggins and Jay McTighe, teacher planning has traditionally been characterized by its focus on the learning activities rather than on the long-term goals, administrators need to attend to the actual learning activity to make sure it is not just for fun—that, by design, a focus is on making meaning and transfer (Wiggins & McTighe, 2005). The task(s) students are asked to perform is the component we need. In other words, we need to ask ourselves: if I were in that classroom, once presented with the task, what would I be able to do that I could not do before (City, Elmore, Fiarman, and Teital, 2009)? We have all witnessed teachers trying cute activities in which the kids had fun but at the end of the day when we asked the student, "so what did you learn?," no "so what" exists—no meaning-making or transfer occurred toward a deeper understanding of content, just perhaps the statement: "it was fun." That is not to say that we are against fun. Quite the contrary, we want every learning moment to be engaging, to have purpose leading to making meaning so that we increase the likelihood that students will retain what they learn and can actually transfer it to a new and/or different context. Thus, it must go beyond mere fun.

We want to prevent what we call the "platter theory" of learning. On Mondays the students come to school with an empty platter "ready to learn." They memorize what the teacher is "covering" so that on Friday, they can "regurgitate" the learning, empty the platter, and be able to return to school the following Monday with an empty platter once again, only to repeat this cycle. This is, of course, intended as an exaggeration, but how far from the truth is it? How many college courses that teachers take employ the same techniques, and even though they made an A for the course, how much of the content knowledge do they transfer into classroom practice? This process may have worked in the past, but it is no longer a viable consideration. The urgency to cover content remains a strongly held belief for teachers because they think that having "covered" the material will better prepare students for state tests. Actually, as Grant Wiggins says, "many of the items that students miss on state tests are transfer tasks" (Wiggins, 2008). Students who just memorize the material have no tools to handle a transfer task. They have no deep understanding of the content, nor do they have the ability to discern when to use or discard what they have learned to solve problems.

In preparation for the Collegial Learning Walk, it is also essential to have a good idea of what to expect and what the teacher expects the outcome of his/her lesson to be. To look for evidence of learning, we need a context. What is the teacher's intention? It is up to the building administrator to translate for team members the plan on paper into planned activities. In other words, the team does not need to "see" the plan. The building administrator describes what is intended and what the administrator expects to see. A word of caution is needed here. Teachers can have a perfect lesson plan, linked to the standards and addressing the key components, but the executions could be disastrous. We have all had those nightmare experiences. We planned things to go one way, but for some reason they do not work out that way. If we reflect on the point at which the plan did not match the actions in the classroom, we can, with mediation from a colleague, analyze what happened and, hopefully, plan to avoid the disaster if and when we implement the same plan again.

Whatever we do, we must never, by design, take a team into the classroom of a teacher we know is in trouble with instructional delivery. Teachers who are in need of serious help should receive intensive assistance until the administrator deems it necessary to move for dismissal. Those teachers' classrooms are not conducive to learning and promoting collegiality. We also do not visit substitutes or teachers whom we know are administering an exam. We want to be able to see the learning process in action, and we NEED to talk to the students. As we prepare to actually go into classrooms, we need to put teachers at ease. They need to know that it is a voluntary process, that it is non-evaluative, and that it promotes the learning of the people on the walk. We want to remind teachers that together we are learning about learning and developing some common understandings we can build upon as we expand our repertoire and actually experience different learning scenarios.

At the school level some basic steps will help everyone focus. Our main intention for the rest of this chapter is to recognize the preliminary thought processing and planning that might take place to set the stage for successful implementation of the Collegial Learning Walks. It is also designed to help administrators establish a common dialogue and reach consensus about what the best in student learning looks like in the classroom. For example, long before the team ever goes on a walk, the principal has requested that teachers let him/her know the answers to the following questions.

Which students are not meeting the state standards?

This information should be readily available in light of the mandated testing programs in place. Principals need to do whatever possible to make this data easily accessible to teachers and readily understood. Students who are not meeting state standards need to be identified as soon as state test results become available. If the data needs to be disaggregated, school building principals need to provide it to teachers in a timely fashion.

What are we doing to help students meet the standards?

Once the teacher knows the student's areas of deficiency, the teacher needs to formulate a plan to address the problem. This cannot be left to chance or made the responsibility of "another" teacher in the building. If the child is in the teacher's classroom, the problem exists within and must be addressed there. It is not someone else's problem. If several teachers are working with the same students, the principal needs to provide time to allow the children's teachers to discuss the problem and plan the remediation and intervention so that no one is wasting time or duplicating efforts. Time spent on meaningful learning is too precious to waste.

Which students understand most of what they read?

This question presupposes that every teacher has tried to assess the reading level of all students. It also presupposes that knowing the reading levels matters because the teacher is going to teach students how to engage in making meaning that leads to transfer with text. Too often, outside a reading class, we simply assign text and expect students to learn from it. If we are not deliberately teaching reading as a subject, we have told ourselves that we are not reading teachers, and that that is someone else's responsibility. In fact, we have learned to compensate for the students' inability to comprehend text by providing them with study guides, worksheets, and other tools to "help them get the gist of the meaning." In effect, we have taken ourselves off the hook and found a way to rationalize not worrying about literacy. Surely, someone else will address it, right? Once a child is out of a self-contained setting, the responsibility for literacy is now distributed among *all* teachers involved. Is it not the reading or language arts teacher's responsibility? The math teacher is there to teach math; the science teacher teaches science, and so on. Yet our graduate literacy reports are giving us a different story. In fact, over time we have come to believe that we learn to read in K-3 and read to learn in grades 4-12. The truth is that we do both all through life.

A simple and useful tool to help everyone in the building assume an internal locus of control concerning literacy development follows (Guilott, Parker, pp. 231-248). It is especially important for content-area teachers to use this tool throughout the year to ensure that students can comprehend what they are reading. A simple school-wide schema to use in determining which students understand what they read follows:

R1 Readers	have trouble with sounds and letters;
R2 Readers	have trouble with words;
R3 Reader	can read every word fluently but do not understand what they read;

A VALUE ADDED DECISION

R4 Readers can read and understand what they read and have internalized strategies to figure out when something does not make sense.

Regardless of the method used to assess the student's ability to "read," this schema will give everyone an easy way to determine how to organize a task that requires reading of text. It is important to note that at any given point any one of us (fluent R4 readers) can become R2 or R3 readers, depending on the text. If we had an auto mechanic's manual and were asked to fix a problem in the car, we probably would become an R2 or R3 reader. Or, if we had a medical book and were asked to explain the cause of an illness in our own words, we would probably turn into an R2 or R3 reader as well. If a student has no prior knowledge of the content, reading text becomes an arduous task. Remember that the informed speaker of a language can use word order and basic syntax to answer questions at a literal level. Following is an example using some nonsense words.

On December 10, 2009, Oogly Pident *plumped* the *frisple* over the *stumor igly because he was utomized to the pupplet. Tuckily, Oogly's muket got* wackeled in the *bozol* on Tuesday, just two days before the *pomple*. How *kumple* Oogly will be when he *fopples* the *frisple* again! Good for Oogly.

Now can we answer the following questions?

When did Oogly plump the frisple?

Why did he plump the frisple?.

What got wackeled?

HOW IS THE INTENTION FOR THE OUTCOME CRITICAL?

Where did it get wackeled?

Will Oogly be happy when he fopples the frisple?

What do you predict Oogly will do next?

Now, let us determine how well we did if this had been our test.

When did Oogly plump the frisple? *On December 10, 2009*

Why did he plump the frisple? <u>*Because*</u> *he was utomized to the pluppet.*

What got wackeled? *Oogly's muket got wackeled.* (word order)

Where did it get wackeled? *In the bozol* (object of the preposition in)

Will Oogly be happy when he fopples the frisple? *Yes, because of the comment: good for Oogly.*

What do you predict Oogly will do next? *This is the question you won't be able to answer. However, one wrong out of six gives the student an 83%.* **The student passes, and the teacher is happy because the student "gets it"—or does he?**

Students need a context to be able to make sense of text. **All** teachers need to provide that context across the curriculum and not assume that because students are fluent readers that they can understand what they read. Therefore, principals need to support literacy across the curriculum in theory and in practice. The collegial learning walks will alert the teachers on the walk to this critical issue.

How has the teacher prioritized the curriculum?

Once again, this question presupposes that the teachers and the principal have had meaningful conversations prior to the opening of school that centered on students' needs, curriculum requirements, and teachers' adaptation and differentiation of instruction that meet the specific needs of all learners. A common mistake is assuming the students do not know anything. With that erroneous belief as the point of departure, coverage of content from A to Z is the actual plan. No prioritization exists, and time becomes the enemy. If the principal and the teachers are able to discuss the teachers' plans for the year, the likelihood of prioritization and differentiation increase tremendously. By virtue of having these conversations, the principal and the teachers become partners. Both parties know what to expect. Without this conversation, assumptions prevail on both parts. Teachers will continue to believe that "covering the content" is what the principal expects and will proceed accordingly: probably documenting the exact page numbers covered and writing them in their lesson plan books. However, if the principal and the teachers come to an agreement about curriculum prioritization, the latter will feel supported and be more likely to become fully engaged instead of being merely compliant, victims of the system and the "curriculum." Getting that internal locus of control is essential if every teacher is going to venture to meet the needs of the students.

Having taken care of these critical points in advance, teacher preparation for going on the Collegial Learning

Walks is much easier. Teachers recognize the real priorities the principal has set. The "cards are on the table," so to speak, and everyone knows that the focus is on students' learning. The shift has begun from attending to what the teacher is doing to looking for evidence of what the student is learning. The tendency to blame failure on those things outside the school day starts to lessen while collaboration begins to flourish. Teachers begin to realize that sharing, networking, and collaborating can multiply their efficacy and increase their success with students. When debriefing a group of teachers and their principal following a Collegial Learning Walk, the following conversation ensued.

A group of six teachers and two principals who completed a Collegial Learning Walk as part of the Instructional Leadership Center's professional development met to reflect and debrief their experience.

The question we posed to open the conversation was, "What was your experience regarding the process?"

Principal A: "This is my second time to participate in a Collegial Learning Walk, and each time I pick up something more, something better. I know I am too tied to the checklist and need to get away from it. Any teacher can put on a dog and pony show, but when we talk to the students, the story changes."

Teacher A: "I asked myself what I was doing to help students make meaning? Do my students know why they are doing what they are doing? It immediately made me reflect on my own practice as a teacher. Tomorrow I will plan differently."

A VALUE ADDED DECISION

Teacher B: "When we talk to the students, we get immediate feedback about our own teaching."

We asked, "How was the mediation of the conversation? What did that cause you to do?"

Teacher C: "It helped me evaluate myself. Actually, it is a great way of helping each other. This process helps us transfer our own learning into our practice by getting together and talking about it. "

Teacher D: "I agree. It really makes me look at everything in a different way. I want to know, are they getting it— am I doing everything I need to do to help the students engage in making meaning? I have questions about my own practice I want to answer."

We probed a little: "What was it about the process that helped you?"

Teacher E: "It's about the whole picture. I might look at one aspect but someone else looks at something else. Then we compare and get a broader, more complete picture, of the learning. We get someone else's perspective and see how other people see the learning. When we debrief, we get perspectives from the students and from the people on the walk. We are getting the whole picture to help all of us learn."

Principal B: "With this process I feel like I am really seeing more than I would if I were going in by myself. Since we all looked at the same thing, we can all discuss it and know what we are talking about."

Teachers recognize the real priorities for student

learning and begin to share best practices as the shift begins toward teaching that improves student learning. Yet, we are not done. Since the common understanding of what making meaning, transfer and student engagement mean to student outcomes can be developed and related to any school's mission, we felt strongly about creating a vehicle to clarify expectations regarding great instruction. Thus, we have devoted the entire next chapter to what we call the "Boomerang Strategies."

CHAPTER 3

The Boomerang Strategies

*"After every difficulty, ask yourself two questions:
"What did I do right?" and "What would I do differently?"*
—Tracy

One of the problems our research identified is that, as teachers, we do not typically transfer what we learn in a workshop into our practice. We also know that we all need feedback and want to be in charge of our own learning, and we certainly do not like others imposing their ideas on us unless we choose them and recognize them as our own. These findings are critical to help us construct ideas that will actually work and be used by teachers in the classroom.

Another common challenge is trying to come to common understanding about our practice. In education we typically roll out a new concept or program until it becomes a household word, but we fail to commit to and build upon what we already know collectively. For example, we throw out the idea of differentiation and nod our heads in agreement because we know that it needs to be present in all our classrooms. What we fail to do is to have meaningful discussions about what it means in our classrooms and with our students. So, we make assumptions that we are all talking about the same thing, but we really are not. In fact, in a room of ten teachers, if we asked each person to write a paragraph describing differentiation in their classrooms, we would end up with ten different scenarios that have little in common with one another. So how do we begin to address this prevalent problem?

We are going to share a strategy that, if used to create common understandings in groups, will yield a rich and generative conversation and new, but common, understandings. We call the process the **Boomerang Strategies** because they are the strategies we revert to when we go back into the classroom. We may not remember what we learned in the workshop, or find it cumbersome to implement given our current situation, but we are already comfortable with our Boomerang Strategies because they are universally identified. They are the way *we* learned, and we typically emulate our own teachers. So why not make these Boomerang Strategies the best they can possibly be based upon what we already know about learning from our own experiences?

We begin by having a conversation with preferably a small group (6-10) on what acquisition, meaning-making and transfer looks like in our classrooms. How do we know when a student is making his own meaning? How can we tell when the teacher is working with students on transfer? Although deceptively simple, these processes are quite complex and difficult to pinpoint. In fact, that is why we praise a well-behaved classroom full of compliant students on task. From the observer's perspective, the students are "doing" what the teacher expects. Although the students may be doing what they have been asked to do, they may not be "engaged." We delude ourselves into believing that these students are really learning. They are actually just memorizing or "learning it" for the test; they are not taking the learning to transfer for the long term. If we want to see students doing work on their own that will endure beyond the test, we will need to make sure that the work we are providing is challenging, and we will need to change how we deliver instruction so that it is engaging.

After we have had a conversation about acquisition, meaning-making and transfer, we then ask the group to complete the Boomerang Strategies Worksheet. We are going to ask the participants to be learners, to think about what they would need to make the strategies work for them and help them make meaning in their own learning experience. An example of what we may need as learners to make reading text meaning-making leading to transfer is that we have to set our own purpose for reading the text. The teacher can guide us, but we have to decide why we are reading it. After using this worksheet with many different groups including college students, principals, teachers, and physicians, for a total of 295 participants, we found many common responses. For example, typical responses for reading text were: "When I have prior knowledge, "when I can make a connection to what's familiar to me," and "when it is not difficult to read."

We also talk about how a worksheet has gotten a "bad rap" but could really be engaging and also help students make meaning. For example, some typical responses here were "When it pushes me to think, "when it has me doing something real," "when I can get feedback," "when it is part of a larger project," "when it helps me clarify and visualize." Lecture is another strategy that students complain is often not engaging. If the lecturer just lectures and drones on, the attendees may doze. But, we know that we have attended some lectures that were actually engaging. What, then, was it about these that made them engaging? What was it about the work that was engaging? Some typical responses here were "when there is a hands-on activity to accompany the lecture, "when there is time built-in to discuss and process in short intervals," "when the speaker is attention-grabbing and uses multi-media to complement as much as possible." Interesting responses for class discussion, for example, included the following: "When I can speak freely protected from adverse consequences," "when the discussion is driven by a meaningful question or problem," or "when we are encouraged to provide different perspectives."

We allow time for everyone to complete the sheet quietly and ask them to drill down deeply and not just say that it has to be relevant. It is tempting and easy to say that learning has to be "relevant" for us to make meaning and take it to transfer. Obviously, everything needs to be relevant. Although that answer is accurate, it is also a "catch-all" response that does not yield any information because it lacks specificity. What is it that we need as students is the question we want to answer. So, the administrator or facilitator will need to probe and say, "How does it become relevant for you? What needs to happen? What conditions must be present?" When we begin to probe, we start to get a rich set of responses that can serve as our common understandings. No one is telling the group what works. The group is generating answers themselves from their own knowledge and their own experiences as learners. Therein lies the difference. Everyone feels competent because everyone is a learner, and as learners we know what we need. Another side benefit is that by going through the process and sharing what we need as learners, we begin to see how we all really do learn differently and process knowledge in different ways. We begin to see differences in a new light. We begin to see that if we, as successful adults, need this much variety, our students may need even more.

The Boomerang Strategies

Boomerang Strategies

Learner situation	What conditions must be present for you as the learner?
1. When is reading text engagement in making meaning that leads to transfer?	When...
2. When is filling out a worksheet engagement in making meaning that leads to transfer?	When...
3. When is solving a problem engagement in making meaning that leads to transfer?	When...
4. When is talking to a peer engagement in making meaning that leads to transfer?	When...
5. When is classroom discussion engagement in making meaning that leads to transfer?	When...
6. When is listening to a lecture engagement in making meaning that leads to transfer?	When...
7. When is taking notes engagement in making meaning that leads to transfer?	When...

8. When is writing a paper engagement in making meaning that leads to transfer?	When...
9. When is working at the computer or some other form of technology engagement in making meaning that leads to transfer?	When...
10. When is working on a project engagement in making meaning that leads to transfer?	When...
11. When is doing homework engagement in making meaning that leads to transfer?	When...
12. When is making a presentation engagement in making meaning that leads to transfer?	When...

Boomerang Strategies

Once everyone has completed his/her individual sheet, as a faculty we record each item as we talk together in a group. The facilitator is documenting what each person is saying, elaborating, clarifying, summarizing— not repeating what has already been said. The information can be captured electronically or on chart paper for immediate and future reference.

What conditions must be present for you as a learner? Following is a mere sampling of responses from different groups:

When is listening to a lecture engaging in making meaning leading to transfer?	What conditions must be present for you as the learner?
	When the teacher uses visuals and models connections
	When we break for brief collaboration of ideas
	When it is broken into chunks including videos, power points, visuals, discussion, etc.
	When expectations are clear of what follows
	When I need to apply something from the lecture
	When there is interaction
	When the topic is familiar to me
	When the lecturer asks open-ended questions that I will need to answer or think about for myself outside class
	When it features illustrations and examples to help me understand

	When the lecturer tells stories to make it real
	When the lecturer seeks input from the class
	When the lecture offers application to novel situations
	When the lecturer uses humor
	When the lecturer includes appropriate use of technology
	When the lecturer evokes emotion in me
	When I can connect with the lecturer or the lecture

We then ask ourselves what we, as teachers, need to do to make sure that the needs we have identified are addressed in our instructional design. The responses come from our common experiences and will become reminders for our instructional practice. These are not mandates from above or dictated to us by anyone. They are practices that we have ourselves identified from our own knowing and collective experience. Incredible power in the collective wisdom emerges in the discussions that follow. Common themes emerge and great ideas flow, all home grown and commonly understood. Following are some of the responses for lecture as an instructional strategy from one group of participants, along with their corresponding plans to include in their instructional design:

If lecture is part of my instructional design, then:

I will prepare, prepare, prepare, prepare and practice it
I will ask open-ended questions that cause the students to think at a deep level
I will have a backup plan
I will tell stories that make the lecture come alive
I will use humor
I will build elegant power points that include class involvement and group work
I will know my audience
I will include visuals, appropriate use of technology, and pause periodically to elicit group understanding and interaction
I will be real
I will not totally read my notes
I will make eye contact and walk
I will remember what it is like to sit there and listen to me (the mind can absorb what the seat can endure)
I will dress appropriately
I will practice my tone and inflection
I will include group interaction
I will be aware of the physical climate
I will read my audience and remain totally engaged and enthusiastic
I will use names
I will use my human "thermostat" in the room

Using these Boomerang Strategies as a starting point of discussion before beginning the Collegial Learning Walks places everyone in the same mindset. No one is more knowledgeable than anyone else. Collectively we know what we need to do. Our next step is committing to doing it and generating a supportive process for ensuring its success. The collegial learning walks then become the venue to "see" what we have committed to doing.

Implementing all twelve strategies at one time may be too time-consuming. We cannot skimp on the time. It is an investment on the front end that sets the stage for what follows. The process is what works. It takes approximately one hour to do four strategies well. In other words, it takes that long to probe for specificity, to help each other elaborate on what we say, to clarify what we mean, and to make our own meaning. The power again is in the conversation itself where we can, non-judgmentally, describe what works for each person as a learner and translates into instructional practice. We are all learners again. What do we need? We know what we need, and now we know that collectively.

First year teachers from Springbank High School in the Rocky View School System in Canada who participated in the Boomerang Strategies discussion had the following to say about the process.

Teacher A: I found it helpful to be asked to consider what I am doing in the classroom from the perspective of the students. The variety of people involved helped to add additional opinions about what is relevant/engaging for everyone. I found it useful to remind myself that while I am trying to survive each day in the classroom, it would be easier if the students were excited/engaged with what we were doing. I think the key for me is to make sure that, as a student, I would be engaged in the activities.

Teacher B: It was good to hear different strategies that people use in the classroom and also to hear how each of us learns and thinks differently, recognizing that our students would be even more diverse than our small group. It was also nice to know that we could discuss teaching strategies and not be evaluated on recognizing our own flaws, but instead see them and think of how we could fix them to take students to deeper depths of learning.

Teacher C: I will continue to reflect on the discussions we had. I want to keep building my teacher skill-set, and this discussion was a great way to identify things that I can work on. An example of this is how I will really try to break up my talking time and give kids some time to process or apply what we are learning.

Teacher D: We all think we learn in our own little bubble, but really, the things that work for us might also work for our students, so it pays to be aware of that.

One construct to help us see ourselves and identify what we need to do is one that looks at our own level of alertness and information about the learners and the content. If we can self-assess where we are privately, we can then begin to consider the changes we will make in our practice. Following is a grid that asks us to consider which two quadrants best describe where we are.

Alert	Informed
I am aware of the responses of my students, and I am willing to monitor and adjust my instruction, so they can work toward transfer.	I know my content well, have background information on all the students and use it to plan accordingly.
Not Alert	**Not Informed**
I am not aware of how my students are responding and just keep going.	I am uncomfortable with my content and my materials. Or, I do not know my students or what they know.

We must, however, remember to keep in mind that it is not about what is wrong but what is next? If we can be honest with ourselves and own our situations, we are much more likely to seek help or make the shift we need to make to engage our students in meaningful learning as a result of our Collegial Learning Walks.

CHAPTER 4

What are the mechanics of the process?

By three methods we may learn wisdom: First, by reflection, which is noblest; second, by imitation, which is easiest, and third by experience, which is the bitterest.
—Confucius

One common problem when principals first hear of Collegial Learning Walks is that they think they are already doing this and are not thrilled with the results they have had with walkabouts, walkthroughs, etc. Typically, they assume this is just another name for something that has already demanded much of their time and attention. They have already stepped up their observations, and in some cases, have met with teacher resistance and resentment. They have used their checklists, marked what they did not see, and even attempted to address it with the individual teachers in the evaluation process. What they fail to see is that a Collegial Learning Walk is a non-evaluative process that uses no written document whatsoever and that its power is in the mediated and coached conversation that happens immediately after the brief classroom observation.

Before we begin our actual process, we shall review some coaching skills that administrators may want to employ with their teachers. The use of coaching language and dispositions in everyday practice are a powerful way to elicit the best in people. If, as principals, we want teachers to have efficacy, to exercise an internal locus of control, and to become interdependent, reflective learners themselves, as outlined in Cognitive Coaching, by Costa and Garmston, then our modeling of the language of coaching and the behaviors that manifest coaching explicitly will be significant. Although as principals, we may recognize the value of coaching, we also know that it is time consuming. To compound the issue, another dilemma we face is wearing both the evaluator and the coaching hats. This dual role can be troublesome and even cause us to abandon coaching altogether. However, by incorporating the coaching language into the Collegial Learning Walks, we can model, probe, and support deep thinking in an efficient and simple way with 2-4 teachers at a time. Coaching now becomes time efficient without the worry associated with teacher evaluation. The principal can, thus, play a vital and meaningful role in teacher development.

Following is a debriefing of a Collegial Learning Walk with a group using coaching techniques. To illustrate how the use of coaching language impacts thinking, we will highlight the coaching process and its powerful outcomes. We will follow the Collegial Learning Walk debriefing protocol that is discussed in detail later in the text to demonstrate how group thinking unfolds in this generative process. Following a classroom visit in an advanced placement geography class, a group, consisting of the principal and two teachers, engages in the coaching/questioning process.

Principal/Coach: What will you take away that you can use right away?

WHAT ARE THE MECHANICS OF THE PROCESS?

Teacher A: I'll take away the fact that the teacher was allowing the students to gather information in a collaborative group in preparation for what was to follow.

Principal/Coach: **Help me understand** what you will do with that? What will you take into your classroom as a result? *(paraphrasing and building rapport)*

Teacher A: I will remember to build background knowledge by having students gather information together. They were really into it.

Principal/Coach: Is that something you can implement right away into *your existing plan*? *(The positive presupposition here is that the teacher has a plan, and that she is thinking of adjusting it.)*

Teacher A: Yes, I know just how I will try it out in my lesson next week.

Principal/Coach: (looking at Teacher B) What were your takeaways?

Teacher B: That although they were working collaboratively, they all had individual responses.

Principal/Coach: How will you incorporate that into *your existing plan*? *(The positive presupposition here is that the teacher has a plan, and that she is thinking of adjusting it.)*

Teacher B: I have struggled with giving group work because I never knew who was doing the work. Now, I realize that they can collaborate, and everyone can still submit his or her own work. What I liked about it is that the collaboration kept them not just on task but engaged.

Principal/Coach: So you plan to incorporate collaborative group work, is that right? *(Paraphrase for clarification)*

Teacher B: Yes, I do. I want to see how it works for me.

Principal/Coach: What was the teacher enabling the students to do? What was the point of the task students were asked to do?

Teacher A: Research information on how language influences culture.

Principal/Coach: Do you agree?

Teacher B: Yes. The students knew the purpose of the lesson, and most were excited about what they were doing. I heard their excitement in their responses.

Principal/Coach: You say most. What percent is that? *(paraphrasing and building specificity)* What percent was engaged and what percent was just on task or, as Phil Schlechty would say, "strategically compliant"?

Teacher B: It was about 80% engaged and about 20% just on task.

Principal/Coach: How do you know? *(specificity and clarity)*

Teacher B: All the students that I talked with could respond to all my questions and were able to apply it to the future. I think students are completely engaged when they will continue working with or without the teacher.

Teacher A: For me, they have to contribute, be active participants, process and add to the learning if they are engaged. On the other hand, if they are just on task, they will just do what they are told.

Principal/Coach: So, am I hearing a definite distinction between engagement and on task behavior? *(Paraphrasing)*

Teacher A: Yes, I now see a marked distinction.

Principal/Coach: What was it about the work that made it engaging? *(Probing for clarity)*

Teacher A: Well, they were working in groups. There was lots of social interaction.

Teacher B: They could choose what they had to address.

Teacher A: And, they were asking each other deep questions.

Principal/Coach: So, what I hear you saying is that the work was engaging because the students were able to exercise choice; they were working in groups collaborating and interacting and they were, as a result, able to ask each other deep questions. Does that capture it? *(Paraphrasing)*

Teacher B: Yes, at first I thought it was just the teacher who was, but after you asked us about the work, I realize that this is transferable.

A VALUE ADDED DECISION

Principal/Coach: When you say transferable, do you mean that anyone, not just the masterful teacher could do it? (**Locus of control**)

Teacher B: Yes, with a little practice, we can all do it.

Principal/Coach: Did you see evidence of authenticity?

Teacher A: No, I did not see any real life application. It was all academic.

Principal/Coach: So, let me make sure that I am tracking. For you, authenticity means that it has to have some application to real life? (**Paraphrasing**)

Teacher A: Yes, doesn't it?

Principal/Coach: What do you think (looking at B)? (**Withholding opinion and judgment**)

Teacher B: I thought it had to do with the product the student was asked to produce. Isn't that evidence of authenticity?

Principal/Coach: Why don't we explore this a little further to see where it takes us? What has to be authentic? Is it the process or the product? (**Withholding opinion and judgment**)

Teacher B: It could be either or both. They just have to approximate real world.

Principal/Coach: So, how would the teacher accomplish that? (**Probing**)

WHAT ARE THE MECHANICS OF THE PROCESS?

Teacher A: She would have to set it up that way from the start. In fact, the students would need to see the rubric and know what is expected of them.

Principal/Coach: Ok, so you are saying that authenticity also includes the learner knowing where he is headed from the start. *(Paraphrasing)* This is one of those concepts we need to explore further to make sure we have common understandings as a faculty. Let us move on to release of responsibility. Where was it in the snippet we watched?

Teacher A: It was in the "You do; I watch stage." The kids would have been able to do this work with or without the teacher.

Principal/Coach: So what do you think the teacher did to get it to this point? *(Locus of control)*

Teacher B: The teacher must have taught them how to own their learning, which is not easy to do. I would love to know how she did it.

Principal/Coach: That may be an "I wonder question" for the teacher. However, you can have that conversation with her anytime to help you understand how she got them to that point.

Art Costa and Bob Garmston, the co-developers, define Cognitive Coaching as a set of strategies, a way of thinking and a way of working that invites self and others to shape and reshape their thinking and problem-solving capacities and is based upon the following four major propositions:

Thought and perception produce all behavior;

A VALUE ADDED DECISION

Teaching involves constant decision-making;

To learn something new requires engagement and alteration in thought;

Humans continue to grow cognitively.

It is not enough for a person to behave in a certain way; what is important is the thinking behind the behavior. A large part of the role of the principal in a Collegial Learning Walk is based on trust and rapport with the people being coached. At the heart of Cognitive Coaching is the concept that each of us has resources that enable us to grow and change from within. Costa and Garmston call these resources "States of Mind." The principal mediates these "States of Mind," allowing the people on the Collegial Learning Walk to explore and use their inner resources more effectively (Costa and Garmston, 2002).

Keeping the Cognitive Coaching model in mind, following are the steps in conducting a Collegial Learning Walk. **First**, the principal assembles a group of 3-5 people. A learning walk is never done just by the principal or even by the principal with one other person. A group of three is minimal, but five seems to work better. Since it is completely voluntary, the group that is assembled must be willing to meet the agreements of the walk.

Agreements for Participation on a Collegial Learning Walk

1. We are all learners helping each other improve our own skills.

2. No one is "there" yet.

3. We are not here to judge.

4. We are not looking for anything in particular, just "effective" instruction leading to transfer.

5. We record nothing.

6. We refrain from talking to the teacher.

7. We maintain strict confidentiality.

8. We agree that the only thing over which we have control is the quality of the work we provide our students.

Special Considerations for the Administrator

The principal must avoid going into a marginal teacher's classroom. The handling of improvement efforts with a marginal teacher should never be a part of the Collegial Learning Walk. That process should remain in the evaluation domain where it belongs. For obvious reasons, the marginal teacher's performance must be observed and monitored with a possible dismissal as the ultimate consequence. The expected outcomes of a collegial learning walk center on improvement efforts and growth for the participants on the walk, not evaluation of teacher performance. As stated, the marginal teacher's destiny is an urgent matter that needs immediate and intensive action. However, if deemed appropriate, the principal could have a marginal teacher as a member of the Collegial Learning Walk team.

The choice of the classrooms to be visited rests with the

administrator leading the walk. Depending on the climate that already exists in the school, classroom visits can be scheduled or unscheduled. More importantly, the principal needs to allay the fears of the teachers being visited. If there is no tradition for unannounced peer visitations, then all visits need to be carefully planned and the teacher being visited should know about it ahead of time. If at all possible, prior to the visit, we have asked the teacher being observed about his/her intention for the learning episode. The principal can refer to a lesson plan or have a brief conversation with the teacher that helps to clarify what the teacher intends. The principal will provide information about the teacher's intent for the lesson to the group going on the Collegial Learning Walk to help set the context.

There are four fundamental premises that guide the discussion.

The first concerns the stage of the learning process. The group will identify whether the task was leading to acquisition, making meaning or transfer based upon student responses or student work (Wiggins &McTighe, 2008). The second speaks to whether the student is engaged or just compliant, referring to Philip Schlechty's *Profile Elements* (The Schlecty Center, 2009). It is important to note that the student could be engaged in a task that leads nowhere! In that case, at the end of the day for that student, no "so what" emerges. The fact that this activity-centered curriculum leads nowhere is one of the twin sins Wiggins and McTighe have identified as problematic (Wiggins & McTighe, 2008). The third concerns authenticity in the learning process. We talk about building relevancy and making learning authentic but seldom know how to make it actually happen. Having a conversation around this will

WHAT ARE THE MECHANICS OF THE PROCESS?

raise questions and generate ideas that would not happen without the common experience of the observation in the classroom. The fourth is about the release of responsibility, which presupposes that the teacher provides the support on the front end and slowly releases responsibility to the student. If we observe confusion, the teacher probably released responsibility too soon. Of course, we are ultimately looking for the student to have full responsibility and to be in charge of his or her own learning. However, we know that the release of responsibility is "gradual," and we recognize that what we will observe indicates its appropriateness for a given task and a specific student. Thus, before we ever walk into the classroom, the principal reviews everything with the Collegial Learning Walk team. The group needs to understand and adhere to the agreements of the collegial learning walk, the four fundamental premises, and the context of the lesson to be observed.

Second, we step into the classroom. With no paper in hand, the group walks into a classroom. For the first trial, we would recommend that the teachers know the team is coming, understand its intention, and be comfortable with what will occur during the visit. The group will look for evidence of making meaning and transfer, authentic learning, and release of responsibility. It may be that the visuals on the wall offer a key, or that a student says something that triggers an appreciation of making meaning or transfer.

Third, the actual visit itself is brief, approximately five to ten minutes, just long enough to attempt to see what the students are actually "getting" as evidenced by our observation and/or is inferred from the students' responses to the following or similar questions:

A VALUE ADDED DECISION

1. What are you learning?

2. What are you being asked to do?

3. How is this like something you have already learned?

4. What will you do with this?

5. What will it help you do?

6. Why is it important to know this?

Wiggins and McTighe, in their 2007 *Schooling by Design* (pp. 21-22) recommend similar questions. When used in a classroom, questions such as these can point to critical elements leading to understanding and transfer, the purpose of schooling. If students are able to respond to these questions in depth, they are engaged in the learning and are committed to developing that intellectual stamina which will keep them going as the process becomes more challenging.

When we ask *the first question (What are you learning?)*, most students are able to retell what the teacher has told them unless they are totally confused. With this question we can determine the level of student engagement or compliance based on the commitment and enthusiasm in the student's response.

The *second question (What are you being asked to do?)* relates to the students' understanding of the task. The richness of the description also points to the depth and complexity of the task.

The *third question (How is this like something you have already learned?)* addresses the students' needs for building on context and prior learning to enhance their retention and connection to what follows.

The *fourth question* (*What will you do with this?*) is directly connected to the point of the lesson. Is it leading the student to transfer? Does the student understand where it is leading beyond the test on Friday, or the end-of-the-year state test? Is the learning connected to a big idea? Has the task engendered in the student a sense of wonder and inquiry?

The *fifth question* (*What will it help you do?*) is determining whether the student sees the value of the task beyond the test. Does the student know what he will be able to do on his own at a later point with the learned information?

The *sixth question* (*Why is it important to know this?*) is a tough question. If the student is able to answer it with some degree of understanding, she will generate the commitment she needs to stick with the task as it increases in depth and complexity.

If the teacher is engaged in direct instruction, we do not interrupt. We may observe for a few minutes and politely leave the room. Typically, we do not comment on an experience in which the teacher is in "telling" mode. We may go back to that class if the format changes. Ultimately, our intention is to observe, describe, and analyze making meaning and transfer. We will not judge it. If this mode is the prevailing or only mode of instruction for that teacher, and if the administrator has a problem with it because results are not adequate, then he or she must handle the situation using a different approach. In other words, it will probably involve the evaluation tools and processes already in place.

However, walking into direct teaching could be avoided if the principal has the context of the lesson beforehand. We must remember to remain as objective as possible and not engage the teacher in conversation. The focus of the Collegial Learning Walk is on student learning.

As earlier stated, it is also important to look for artifacts that provide evidence in the room of release of responsibility, making meaning, and authentic learning. Often the teacher has "published" student work on the bulletin board or in some other format and has posted support tools for students (rubrics, graphic organizers, test results, reports, projects, stories, etc.). These are worth examining because they, too, tell a story about learning. We look for original student work that is not a repeat for every student in the room. We look for progress assessment and for the conditions in the room that would support making meaning and transfer.

Although it may seem that the students will be distracted and that the flow of learning will be interrupted with 3-5 people entering the room, our experiences have shown that students appreciate that we are showing an interest in them and quickly enjoy the fact that we are asking them about their learning. These 6-7 questions repeatedly asked over time in different classrooms will prompt the students to start questioning the "so what" of what they are learning. Specifically, if they know that other adults will be coming into their classrooms seeking their answers to the same questions, they will begin to try to answer these for themselves. Teachers will also begin to recognize the importance of keeping these questions present in the daily lesson planning. Would it not be great if students could tell us why they are really learning and not just reply "because it is on the test or because the teacher said so"?

WHAT ARE THE MECHANICS OF THE PROCESS?

While in the classroom 5-10 minutes, we strive to capture a glimpse of the learning occurring in the classroom from multiple perspectives. It is as if we were taking multiple video clips of the same event at the same time from different perspectives and analyzing their intersections. We avoid talking to the same students and walk around the room to look for evidence of making meaning and transfer. In so doing, each observer will offer a slightly different view of the experience and the moment. That is the power of the Collegial Learning Walks. It is not about one single person's perspective; it is about a collaborative and integrated picture of the event. Teachers may think that they need to see teaching at their grade level and/or discipline to gain something from the experience. The truth is that learning is learning regardless of the age or subject. In fact, sometimes we are better able to de-personalize the moment if it is not in our area of "expertise." As teachers we may tend to color the experience from our own "expert" position. If we can just stay in the moment, capture what we see, and describe our observations, we will be better able to analyze the learning in relation to the teaching and reflect it back to our own practice.

Fourth, when we step outside the classroom, we immediately look for a quiet corner or place between classrooms where we can debrief the experience. The protocol that follows is the "magic" of the Collegial Learning Walks. The building administrator leading the walk is the one who will ask all the questions and attend to any possibility of the process being derailed. This requirement is essential to maintain the level of trust necessary to prevent teachers from "personalizing" the experience and making it something other than the observation of the learning experience.

A VALUE ADDED DECISION

The **list of debriefing questions** is always the same or very similar to the following. (Note: When just beginning, it is best to use them exactly as written below.)

What did you observe that you could take away immediately?

What was the teacher enabling the students to do? What is the point of the task students were asked to do?

Was the teacher taking the students to transfer? How do you know?

Were the students engaged in making meaning? Did you observe evidence of understanding?

What percent of the students were engaged in making meaning leading to transfer? How do you know? How many were compliant? How do you know?

Did you see evidence of authentic learning? What was it about the work that was authentic?

How was the release of responsibility?

What could the teacher have done to "kick it up a notch"?

Because this debriefing should begin on a positive note, it is best to start by asking the following question: ***What did you observe that you could take away immediately?*** This question has the power of focusing everyone's attention on an aspect of the moment observed that can be replicated. As the old adage goes, "imitation is the highest form of flattery." This is the beginning of the descriptive process that sets the tone for the entire debriefing. Because the group represents multiple perspectives, it is not difficult for one person in the group to identify something that he or she found particularly useful. It may be that everyone in the group finds something different that can be replicated. The answer to this question is the basis for the first point of feedback that the administrator leading the Collegial Learning Walk could give the teacher, if the teacher has asked for feedback. The answer to this question also prompts discussion that will inevitably lead to insightful comments about the observation.

The second question is one that pinpoints the experience immediately. This question is one that Elaine Fink offered in her training: **What was the teacher enabling the students to do?** The intention is to get everyone's descriptive perspective of what the teacher was generally trying to accomplish with the task at hand. The responses are non-evaluative, completely objective, and descriptive of the event. Depending on the experience, by design, the leader of the group needs to get everyone in the group to contribute at this point. In answering this question, the group can sharpen its observational skills as each group member supports, disagrees with or corroborates other group member assertions, which must be supported with evidence. Since group members are not using assessments, the group leader must find a way to keep the discussion descriptive throughout and supported by only the evidence observed, always vigilant that not even a hint of judgment creeps into the debriefing.

The third question refers to the point of schooling: **Was the teacher taking the students to transfer?** With this question the group is making a grounded assessment. To ensure that it is a grounded assessment and not just a

A VALUE ADDED DECISION

superficial assessment, the second part of that question is **"How do you know?"** It is critical that the conversation remain descriptive and de-personalized. The group is looking for evidence of transfer. However, keeping in mind that this observation is very brief, the evidence gathered is also just a snapshot. It merits reiterating that the intention in the debriefing is to describe the learning collectively and the task the student is being asked to do in the context of the teacher's intention for the lesson. We must underscore *collectively*. Responses are layered, offering a mosaic of the experience. The whole issue of the learning stages leading to transfer is grounded in the work of *How People Learn: Brain, Mind, Experience and School* written by the Committee on Developments in the Science of Learning. Thus, if we look at acquisition, making meaning, and transfer as stages in learning, we can readily see that acquisition will be easily identifiable. Making meaning may be easily recognized as well, as long as the student is attempting to make his or her own meaning. Transfer, on the other hand, is not easy to "detect." However, the process pointing to transfer is fairly easy to identify. In the five or ten minutes of the visit, some of the artifacts in the room and the answers from the students can provide us the best information. We know we will probably see students in acquisition stage if the teacher is in didactic mode. However, if the students are working independently or in a group, it is extremely important that we hear from them the answers to the questions, the task each person is doing, and any other information they volunteer once we probe for specificity. The group will find the best evidence of making meaning and transfer in the verbal description the students offer and from the tasks the students are being asked to do. During the walk, it is also important that we look at the task to determine depth and complexity and level of understanding or frustration.

WHAT ARE THE MECHANICS OF THE PROCESS?

The fourth question is also a two-part probe that demands evidence. **Were the students engaged in making meaning? Did you observe evidence of understanding?** The group is looking for engagement in making meaning, not just engagement in mindless drivel that leads nowhere. Using Philip Schlechty's *Profile Elements* of the degrees of engagement, we are looking for engagement, compliance and non-compliance in varying degrees. In the past, if the teacher was getting students to respond to questions, we considered this engagement when, in reality, it was probably merely a form of compliance. Katie Ray Wood explains, "If a teacher primarily asks questions whose answers she already knows, students often learn to respond with a kind of 'worksheet' talk, in which they fill in her blanks and wait patiently for the next question" (Wood, 2006)

If the students are engaged, they will have the necessary commitment to "stick with the task" when it gets difficult. They will not shy away from challenge and will draw from their own creativity. They will have questions they want to pursue and will want to do more. However, students who are compliant will appear on task, may even stick with the task in pursuit of the prize (grade), but will not go beyond what is expected. Seeing that distinction is essential and yet sometimes rather difficult.

When a student is making meaning, he is struggling with the new learning and attempting to own it and evaluate his own ideas. It will appear messy to the observer. In some cases, in their quest to make meaning, students will completely misunderstand. When students verbalize their thought processes, teachers can redirect their thinking when it is off the mark and help them build on what they already know. Teacher redirection cannot happen without frequent formative assessments, probes, and meta-cognitive coaching. Despite concerns about the amount of time spent, giving students the "meaning" accomplishes nothing and perpetuates a dependency on the part of the students. Often, pressed for time, the teacher may weaken and begin giving the students the "answers" to the puzzling problem or challenge. If students do not construct their own meanings and work through them, they will quickly forget what they have learned and never reach transfer. Again, in a didactic classroom, students come to class with that empty platter on Monday, and the teacher fills the platter and gives the students the test on Friday. As previously noted, students will "dump" what they know on the test and, in short order, forget what they supposedly "learned." On Monday when they come back to school their platter is once again empty and waiting to be filled.

The fifth question also refers back to Philip Schlechty's *Profile Elements*: **What percent of the students were engaged in making meaning leading to transfer? How do you know? How many were compliant? How do you know?** At this point we are looking for a number that will help us form a relative perspective of everyone's picture of the situation. By assigning a number, the group members begin to concretize what they have determined to be engagement versus compliance. Although quite unscientific, the intention here is to begin to calibrate each other by sharing reasons for the numbers. This process begins to build specificity into the discussion. For example, if we say that 30% were engaged and 70% were compliant, we have to justify our answer and offer examples and numbers to back up our assertion. In our conversation and scans of the class members, we may have seen six students out of twenty who were just compliant (doodling, working on the page without knowing why, or quietly waiting for direction) and made our 70%

WHAT ARE THE MECHANICS OF THE PROCESS?

prediction based upon the students that we actually questioned or heard during the brief snapshot. A good follow-up question is the following: "What was it about the task that made it engaging? Or, what was it about the task that was not engaging?"

Question number 6 is straightforward and points to the heart of the issue: **Did you see evidence of authentic learning? What was it about the work that was authentic?** Here the group members are reminded that authenticity is critical to promote understanding. The questions that ask the student what will happen with this learning over time are all designed to get at this issue. By probing this way, the process is a reminder of what we might find in a classroom where students are engaged in making meaning and transfer. Generally speaking, we talk about the need for relevancy and a connection to the real world but never quite get what that might look like in a real classroom with real students. This is the opportunity to look for it in action, to capture the moment, and to let it spark other authentic learning possibilities for the observers as they reflect on their own teaching. It is also an opening to talk about what makes it authentic or what does not make it authentic. In other words, it is a real chance to clarify what we mean by authenticity and to network other possibilities, even if not present in the classroom just observed.

Question number 7 reminds the group to look for the gradual release of responsibility filter: *How was the release of responsibility?* Here the group is looking for the effects of everything the teacher has done to prepare the students to move toward independence. Typically, teacher support will be evident in many different ways ranging from verbal and visual cues to graphic organizers, grouping patterns, mediation, and coaching. This filter is critical as the group begins to identify the stage of learning for the student. In a classroom that appears to be totally student-directed, the teacher has put in place a series of steps and practiced these to ensure the smooth transitions that characterize a totally student-centered environment. To the novice teacher, arriving at this point may seem like a daunting task, but it will be important to discuss what supports, routines, and procedures are in place to ensure that the process in which students are engaged leads to making meaning and transfer. Just having students working independently or in groups is not enough—they must know what they are learning, when they will use it, how they will use it and why they are learning it.

The last question, or number 8, is incredibly powerful for the group because it causes everyone to focus and think analytically about the experience: **What could the teacher have done to "kick it up a notch"?** At this point in the mediated discussion, the group has analyzed what they just observed or heard. Each person has offered his or her own non-evaluative perspective on the brief visit. Now, it is time to consider what might have made it more engaging, leading to making meaning and transfer for all students. Responses here will vary, and the leader needs to honor what each person offers but guard against evaluation seeping into the process. Since a premise of the Collegial Learning Walks is that everyone can improve, then talking about possibilities fits perfectly and complements the discussion with "what if." By just asking this question a presupposition emerges that means, no matter how well a lesson went, as we self-reflect, we need to consider how we could have improved upon it. Besides helping the team members learn about learning together, the Collegial Learning Walks encourage self-reflection. This question alone prompts the self-reflective message as critical in the process, almost like an unobtrusive reminder of what best practice looks like in action. It is from the responses to this question that the principal gathers the suggestion to give to the teacher requesting the feedback. The principal needs to consider the suggestions and make sure that whichever one s/he offers is legitimate and will indeed improve an aspect of learning in that classroom.

If the teacher visited wants feedback, we provide a couple of ways to do it that work quite well. One way is just to give the teacher the same questions that the group answered and have the teacher self-reflect before providing any kind of feedback. A second step or a quick way is simply to tell the teacher the following:

"Here is takeaway..." which would come directly from responses to the first question. Hearing that other teachers have found something they can imitate in their classrooms is gratifying to know.

"We wondered about..." would allow for non-evaluative questions the group may have posed during the process.

"Here is a suggestion..." comes from the final question asked and presupposes that everyone can improve, even the master teacher.

However, the principal must always be the one who provides feedback to the visited teacher. Other members of the Collegial Learning Walk will refrain from giving any sort of feedback to the teacher. An initial agreement for the entire faculty should be that feedback will be sought from only the principal, never from a member of the walk.

CHAPTER 5

How is every member of the Collegial Learning Walk a learner?

"I'm a Learner, too:
Learning About Learning Together"

Wisdom begins in wonder.
—Socrates

By virtue of becoming a learner again, everyone on the learning walk gives up the role of evaluator. The group's commitment is to learning together about learning. Firmly establishing the role of learner for everyone puts every member on a level playing field. Nobody is the keeper of the secrets. The tacit assumption is that everyone knows a great deal and that sharing that knowledge has immense value and transferability. Another assumption is that we each have something to gain from the entire process whether in the classroom observing, or talking to the students, or in the debriefing session sharing what we separately gained, or talking about insights we now have. Given that our cup is not yet filled with knowledge, each participant is open to new possibilities. Adhering to the purity of the intention of the Collegial Learning Walk is essential if the process is going to work effectively. Members of the learning walk will be credentialed, experienced, knowledgeable, and wise. Yet, each learning walk is a learning experience, with something new to be gained and the possibility of understanding learning at a deeper level with all the intricacies that go into the skill, joy, and art of teaching.

Each experience is in a different context but with a common purpose. We all want to develop understanding and help the students, in turn, develop the ability to retrieve what they have learned in a new and different context when a new situation warrants. Therefore, what we share constitutes our quest for what makes our instructional practice result in increased student learning. We have managed to identify the routines and procedures that work well in classroom management. We are now looking for what teachers do to engage the learner in making meaning leading to transfer. We are not looking for a teacher's "dog and pony show" which demonstrates compliance on the part of the students; we are looking for the nuances of our instructional practice that are difficult to describe and demonstrate in any setting other than the moment in the classroom.

To obtain qualitative data to prove the effectiveness of the Collegial Learning Walks, we conducted an interview with Leslie Collins, principal of Springbank High School in Alberta, Canada, which revealed the learning experience this process afforded new teachers in the school.

US: How would you describe a collegial learning walk to someone who has never participated in one?

Leslie: It is a generative, collaborative process that is about the learning of the people on the walk. It is one of the best instructional leadership opportunities for administrators. It is a way to provide instructional leadership.

US: After participating on three collegial learning walks, you said it was career changing. What do you mean?

Leslie: I struggled with how to be an instructional leader. I did not know how to go about doing it and giving appropriate feedback. It was shallow. It did not have context. It was something I have struggled with through my whole administrative career. When I went on a Collegial Learning Walk, I realized that the more people you have going on a learning walk throughout the year, the more generative, the richer and deeper the feedback I can provide. It's so much better than what I alone can provide.

I like that the process is non-judgmental. It feels like it is what it is intended to be, which is to be helpful, a learning process for everyone involved. It is an excellent way of providing feedback and giving teachers something that is worthwhile for them. On a CLW we force people to find something worthwhile for themselves. But you are ***not*** forcing your own judgment on them. I like the idea of talking to kids because it is the only way to find out if they are making meaning leading to transfer. We cannot see it unless we ask.

US: What would you recommend to an administrator planning to conduct Collegial Learning Walks?

Leslie: I would say...

...Do *not* use it for an evaluative purpose because as soon as you do, it is game over.

...Start small, preferably with new teachers as part of their induction process. I am trying to grow it in a grassroots way and use it purposefully.

A VALUE ADDED DECISION

...It is for your own professional development, for you to become a better instructional leader and to help all involved to better understand and intentionally plan for student learning. The assumption is that no one has *the* answer. We are all learning together, truly building a community of learners.

... I would keep it small and grow it strategically.

US: How did you start?

Leslie: I started with new teachers in my building.

US: How did you approach them?

Leslie: I talked to them about coming into their classrooms. We sat down and talked about what they wanted the focus to be. I told them that the process would be nonjudgmental and that I was working on becoming a better instructional leader. I did not get too specific. I also told them that the process is intended for the people on the walk to become better at their craft. I told the new teachers that if they wanted feedback, they could ask me.

US: How did you give them feedback?

Leslie: I asked them most of the questions that we had debriefed.

What were you enabling the students to do?

Were you taking them to transfer? How do you know?

What percent of the students were engaged in making

meaning? What percent were compliant?

What could you have done to "kick it up a notch?"

US: What were their responses?

Leslie: Some of their responses were thoughtful, and some were shallow. I had to work on the ones that were shallow through coaching. That immediately allowed me to pinpoint for them areas that needed their attention. They knew my intention was to help them. For example, when I asked one teacher about engagement in making meaning in a class where we had observed a whole group discussion with two students talking and the rest doing nothing, we were able to talk in a non-judgmental way about possibilities for group engagement instead of having just a small number participating. Many discussions were centered on making meaning leading to transfer.

I had never had this kind of conversation until I did the Collegial Learning Walks. It was honest, helpful, and real. It just gets to a different level. Our conversations are not about what is wrong; they're about what is next. I invite them to talk about what we can do to fix it. Also, what I like about the conversation with the group is that it is non-judgmental. You are not in the spotlight; you are engaging in dialogue. The conversations are generative, particularly for our own teaching and learning. The teachers on the walk take what we are talking about and apply it to their own situations. I have seen the people on the walk start asking the right questions about their own needs. They begin to self-reflect during the mediated conversation. For example, the drama teacher I took on the walk wanted to go into the PE class to see engagement in a non-academic environment to improve her own work. The new math teacher that went on the walk met with the English teacher about Socratic seminars. The English teacher asked the math teacher to join her assessment team to assess her Socratic seminar.

So you get a cross pollinating of existing silo structures and begin to break the barriers down. A math teacher wanted to go into another math teacher's classroom. I encouraged him to go into a non-math teacher's class where he might pick up a different pedagogy. I convinced him to see that it is about the students, not just about the content.

US: I know that research tells us that we lose a large percentage of our teachers in the first few years. It looks like you have found a way to change that.

Leslie: If they do not stay, it's not because I did not try. In the past, it was sink or swim for the new ones. Some sank and did not swim. If they do not know what you need to see, they are never going to hit it. You can try the teacher documents with all the indicators but you will overwhelm them. This process is nice and tight. We work on specific doable bits and pieces as needed to get the students to making meaning and transfer.

The process walks the talk about assessment and setting people up for success and giving them opportunities to practice. Then, when you do go into the "evaluation," nothing is a surprise. Therefore, I cannot emphasize enough that you **cannot** use it as an evaluative piece. It has to be formative.

US: Why did you start with new teachers?

Leslie: I picked them because I knew they would not be resistant. Then when I went on a learning walk with a first year teacher, I assured him that the walk is as much for my learning as for his. When I approach the more experienced teachers, I also let them know that it's about their learning, my learning, and they automatically open the doors. But, my intention has to be pure.

For the first time ever I feel like I am doing my job. This is how I can become an instructional learning leader. This is not about the requisite three evaluations. Now, I can go to sleep and believe that I am doing a far better job of doing what I need to do with my teachers.

It is amazing how it all falls into place. When you do it this way, everything falls into place. The measure of a process is in how many different ways it can go. This process goes in so many different, energizing directions. The only way it can go wrong is if you take any of it out of context and try to use it in isolation.

As a principal, I have to take my ego and store it in my desk because if I come to the table and use this process to lord over teachers, it will not work. But if it is truly a part of my growth plan, and I convey that I want to learn from them, it goes much farther. If you can check that ego into the desk drawer, and let staff know that you are trying to improve, that goes a long way.

US: How is this working for you day to day?

Leslie: I had to put a few things on the back burner to make this work. I had to ask myself what I was willing to give up. Most of it, I cannot tell you what it was, obviously did not matter. I am focusing on what matters most, our collective learning.

CHAPTER 6

What are some of the possible steps in the implementation process?

Do not go where the path may lead, go instead where there is no path and leave a trail.
—Ralph Waldo Emerson

The answer to this question is totally contextual. The principal has to make that call based upon whether teacher and administrative expectations are the same. If the prevailing school culture is one of mistrust and one-upmanship, then Collegial Learning Walks would not be a place to start. On the other hand, if the culture supports collegial conversations, if a collaborative spirit prevails, not competitive or adversarial, and if a clear focus on improvement is evident, Collegial Learning Walks as a process will thrive. Collegial Learning Walks are a professional development model designed to support the learning for the people on the walk. Following are some possible beginning points:

- Become comfortable with the mediation of the group's learning by participating in learning walks as a member of the team first, then as the leader of the group.
- Make sure that teachers understand the intention of the Collegial Learning Walks. If you are in your own school, talk one-on-one to the teachers whose classrooms you will visit and show them what you plan to

A VALUE ADDED DECISION

do. Ask them if they want feedback.
- Print out the Agreements, the questions to ask the students, and the debriefing questions, so that everyone participating knows the protocol that will be used. Review the Agreements, and remind everyone not to engage the teacher in dialogue during the visit.
- Invite teachers on a voluntary basis to go on a Collegial Learning Walk. Try to include the "speed boat" teachers and those highly regarded by their peers in the school for the first learning walk. Build in a method that will provide you timely feedback of the process.
- Use the feedback information to make adjustments in how you proceed.
- Before you take anyone on a learning walk, spend 30-45 minutes with the whole group talking about why you are doing this, what you hope to accomplish, and what will actually happen. Make sure you leave an opening for their questions and concerns. Address them as they come, but make certain that you build in the enthusiasm for the experience and the entire process.
- Stress again and again that this is a professional development model for the people on the walk, not a quality control strategy.
- Remind everyone that the process is non-evaluative and make sure all members know what that means.
- After leaving each classroom, we walk down the hall away from the classroom we just visited, find a quiet spot and begin our debriefing session. It is best if you can debrief each visit in a small quiet and private area where you can sit and think.
- At the end of the first learning walk event, after you have conducted and debriefed at least four classroom visits, ask everyone to reflect on the process before

WHAT ARE SOME OF THE POSSIBLE STEPS?

  disbanding and share it with the group. You will have a really good sense of its effectiveness based on this particular conversation.
- Before you create a second team, review the first group's experiences with a colleague and make the necessary adjustments to ensure programmatic success. Since it will be helpful to take the first group on a second walk, schedule that time before taking another group on a Collegial Learning Walk.
- Some school administrators will take their groups to another school in the district to avoid the possibility of judgment from peers. That is definitely a principal's prerogative.
- Initially, the scheduling of learning walks is a big decision because of the fear of disrupting the learning process. That is simply not true. What you will gain will more than compensate for the few minutes the group is in each classroom. Typically, principals schedule learning walks once or twice a month. Once teachers see the value, the process becomes a continuous learning, job-embedded, and research-based model for professional development.

To summarize, before beginning the learning walks with teachers, an administrator must ponder the answers to the following question to determine his or her readiness for such a powerful undertaking: *How do I know when I am ready to take teachers on a collegial learning walk?*

1. I have gone on several CLWs with peers in which someone coaches me on the debriefing process.
2. I have seen CLWs work first hand, and I support the process wholeheartedly in conversation with others.

3. I have developed keen listening skills and know how to redirect, paraphrase, clarify, promote an internal locus of control,* probe for clarity and specificity, and build on positive presuppositions about the teacher's behavior.
4. I have made the purpose of the CLW crystal-clear to the teachers visited and to the members of the team on the walk, distinguishing the process from supervisory walk-throughs.
5. I am a keen observer of what is going on in the classroom and know how to tune out the teacher to watch kids closely.
6. I am able to "protect" teachers verbally against any judgment or criticism that might creep in, even casually.
7. I have built a strong element of trust with everyone involved in the CLW.
8. I have made the time allocation for CLWs a priority so that I do not abandon the process mid-stream unless a true emergency develops.
9. I am ready, willing, and able to learn something new every day with the teachers on the walk. I never tire of the process.
10. I self-reflect on a regular basis to ensure that I honor this protocol.

* People with internal locus of control believe in their own efficacy to make things happen; people with an external locus of control believe that they have little control over what matters in their lives or workplace.

CHAPTER 7

How is the process synergy in action?

What we learn with pleasure, we never forget.
—Alfred Mercier

It has been our experience that when teachers reflect on the questions in the mediated conversations, they begin to see possibilities in their own classrooms and situations. Ideas begin to intertwine and an informal networking system develops. This system could be supported electronically through the creation of a social network for the teachers where instructional practice can thrive. Additionally, the ideas evolve as a peer coaching model emerges voluntarily and seemingly spontaneously. When these possibilities take form, the principal needs to find a way to support it, encourage it, and keep it going. The Collegial Learning Walk process will re-ignite the flame that initially got us into the teaching profession. The administration needs to find ways to feed that flame as it shapes a solid professional culture that examines current practice from the learner's perspective. The process capitalizes on what is next, pushing toward constant and continuous improvement.

In an interview with Kim Brandon, Principal of Northeast Middle in St. Louis, Missouri, examples of synergy in action can be readily isolated.

A VALUE ADDED DECISION

US: How would you describe a Collegial Learning Walk to a colleague?

Kim: It is not a walkthrough or a drive-by, as teachers say. A walkthrough implies you are looking for things and walking through. A Collegial Learning Walk means you have the opportunity to learn and to learn from one another. Everyone in the group is a learner.

US: What convinced you to try the Collegial Learning Walks?

Kim: I thought I had already done them, but the tipping point for me was when you took teachers through the activity of envisioning through the eyes of a learner. How do we learn? How do we design our instruction so that we can meet the expectations of us as learners? What must be happening in our current classrooms? There must be something else. That was the "tipping point" for me.

The year before, as a staff, we had worked to create a walkthrough checklist, and we identified what we wanted to see and connected it to our learning principles. Administrators started going into classrooms with the checklist. I knew right away it did not work, but I was unwilling to let it go. What we realized is that it was not simple to look for strategies in a classroom. We tried to gather data about what we saw and did not see. Teachers began getting suspicious, and I'm not sure what data we were gathering. It was not doing us any good. Still I persisted and tried different things. We left the marked checklist of skills with the teachers. They started to question what we were doing and pointing out what we had failed to observe and check off. So we tried something else. I started leaving feedback. However, it, too, was hollow and empty. The checklist did nothing to identify the learning. Fortunately, school ended, and I had the opportunity to catch up on summer reading and reflection. I finally realized I had to scrap the checklist. It was embarrassing to say it was just wrong. Marzano had written an article that made fun of what I had done with "my high yield strategies." He pointed out that these might work with one group and not with another. I realized I had to do something else and just not do the walkthrough checklist any more.

US: How did you begin?

Kim: First, I had to accept that I had to get rid of what I had been doing. I had to be honest with the staff. I told them this was one of my blind spots— that I tried to make it work even though I knew it wasn't working. I shifted my focus and told them that what we wanted to do instead was look at what our students are doing. I turned to the work we had done as a staff about what engaging in making meaning leading to transfer looks like and what we knew had to be in place. After doing that exercise and reflecting on it, people felt competent right away. We all started in the same place. All of us knew what had to be there. It was not my telling them anything or Marzano telling them anything. We had figured it out together using the Boomerang Strategies (See CHAPTER 3). No matter who you are as a teacher, you know what it takes to be a learner. We compared it to the research studies we had and realized we did know some things. If we know this to be true, and we do not see it, then how do we make it happen? In what are the students engaged, and how do we know? As we continued to build our competence to better engage the students, we grew together.

US: In other words, although I believe there is a place for the checklist, it alone did not work. Last year you and your administrative team identified what you wanted to see on a checklist. This time the entire group generated what you needed as learners, and you did not put it on a checklist.

Kim: Now, we do not take the checklist, we take the understanding. As I said, before we started the Collegial Learning Walks (CLW), we shifted our thinking. We did the Boomerang Strategies exercise with the whole staff in small groups to welcome conversation and deepen understanding. We carved that time into the first month of school. It was an investment up front. Then, after you coached us, we practiced as an administrative CLW team. We needed to be coached the first time, and we each had to be participants first and not facilitators. We had to fill the participants' shoes first to become better leaders ourselves.

US: Was that so that you would understand how hard the task really was and to avoid being judgmental?

Kim: Yes, it is not easy to answer the questions in the protocol. For example, we recognized that the level of engagement depended on who was observing whom. Each one of us had a different perspective to bring to the conversation. Equally important was taking turns facilitating and coaching each other. We went through the whole process as we did the debriefing, and toward the end, we asked each other what felt good and what did not feel good. In that way, we were able to help each other become confident and competent in the process. We actually practiced releasing responsibility. Now each of us facilitates the group of teachers we evaluate. We have put collegial learning walks on rotation. Every Wednesday we have built in the CLW.

HOW IS THE PROCESS SYNERGY IN ACTION?

In other words, each week administrators are engaged in learning walks.

US: So you have built in a process for enhancing leadership capacity among your administrative team that will have a ripple effect with the teachers. How are you feeling now about the process?

Kim: I notice that as we get comfortable, we are getting better at guiding and asking probing questions, better at coaching. People are now more comfortable talking to students and much more engaged in the debriefing. Teachers whose classrooms we go into do not want to wait. They want the feedback right away. They take it and use it. Now we have added the lens of the release of responsibility. They saw value in how it impacts learning, releasing too soon or not releasing at all. As the process evolves, we have started going into other content areas, not just the one we teach. Doing that forces the teacher to engage with the strategy. I call it our cross–pollination. They are connecting with one another at much higher levels than ever before.

US: What would you recommend to a principal thinking about learning walks?

Kim: You don't rush into it. It's important to take staff through the Boomerang Strategies. It was a catalyst for us. Once we did it together, we were all on the same page. We were all learners in an engaging and meaningful experience. We were very explicit. Then we could compare our indicators with our learning principles.

You have to know that your administrative team is on the same page. You have to trust your administrative team

A VALUE ADDED DECISION

implicitly. If one of the team members goes out and creates distrust or violates the protocol, you will lose the whole school. We come together and talk about the process on a regular basis. It energizes us.

US: Kim, talk about the trust factor.

Kim: Trust is huge. The first time I took one of my "Mavens" (from Malcolm Gladwell's *The Tipping Point*) on a learning walk. I had identified the Mavens in my building, the people whom everyone respects, the go-to people, and asked one of them to go on something called a Collegial Learning Walk after we had done our work on the Boomerang Strategies. After participating in one, she told me right away, "This is really good." Seriously, the first group went through, and it was not scary.

US: In other words, like everything new, she wondered how it would affect the teachers and was positively impressed.

Kim: But she was also prepared to listen and, most importantly, people trust her. The nice thing is that she was my Paul Revere. In "The Tipping Point" Gladwell says that other people had warned that the British were coming but that it was Paul Revere's word that the patriots heeded because they trusted him. You need that person/s who will be honest with you and tell you the truth. She was my Maven. Here is the fascinating thing about the Maven factor. The teachers trust them even though they know that the Mavens talk to me. You need to know who they are in your building and foster those relationships.

US: You have a big school so you definitely need Mavens. Given your huge faculty, you have found other ways to

HOW IS THE PROCESS SYNERGY IN ACTION?

connect with your staff. Talk about the internal follow-up for your 100-plus teachers, the Friday Flyer, a professionally done electronic newsletter.

Kim: My Friday Flyer is a reflection of the week and sets the stage for what we will be doing the next week. I try to find things that we are working on as a staff, but break it up into little stories that are easy to digest, rather than a whole article. I've also learned that I can go back and talk about the same thing again and, each time, I pick up someone else. I know that my teachers get it when they are ready. So, I don't judge them. I support them until they are ready. In other words, each week I write a letter in my Friday Flyer and have a private conversation with the teachers.

US: You have other information in The Friday Flyer that supports the work you are doing in your building and keeps everyone informed in a quick and efficient manner.

Kim: If I am struggling, I do not pass judgment. I own the problem. Instead of getting mad, I try to own it. I ask myself: How can I reflect this in a way that people will hear it? I never want to assume that I am the expert. What I will do is get the resources, read a lot and try to bring them information to help them. Each week it hits someone differently. I try to personalize the work. I value time so I do not waste their time when we come together.

US: In other words, when you do get together as a faculty, your meetings are not about administrative matters, they are about what really matters, the learning in your building.

Kim: I care about my teachers, and I want them to

succeed. I know sometimes I make them mad, but they keep rising to the occasion.

US: You set high standards and are growing a professional instructional culture.

Kim had the courage to abort her checklist walkthrough method of evaluation and to try the Collegial Learning Walks with her teachers. Through this generative process, she has been able to create true learning teams that are ever cognizant of ways to increase students' depth of knowledge and ensure they will truly remember what they have learned. In addition, the teachers are now more able to differentiate their instruction to help ensure that all students are moving from acquisition, to making meaning, then to transfer of their knowledge.

CHAPTER 8

How is the process a continuous growth model?

Education is not the filling of a pail, but the lighting of a fire.
—William Butler Yeats

The experience teachers get from the Collegial Learning Walks is both enlightening and unsettling. Everyone will get a few insights to take back, but mostly it will prompt a few self-reflective questions that will have an impact on their actual plan and delivery of instruction. At the beginning of the process the principal leading the walk needs to be gentle with the questions and pull back on probing to avoid any feeling of judgment. However, as teachers going on the walk repeat the process, the leader of the walk can begin to probe for specificity and help teachers clarify their thinking and assumptions. In other words, the process will become progressively more rigorous as teachers experience confidence building and success. Since it is a non-evaluative model, the feedback the visited teacher gets is not the focal point. The growth builds from the conversations on the Collegial Learning Walk that pinpoint issues which would not surface otherwise. By addressing concrete as well as elusive aspects of the learning process, everyone begins to make their own meaning that they, too, will transfer into their own classrooms.

It will be tricky for administrators to stay true to the non-evaluative nature of the process. Because time is so precious, administrators will want to incorporate the learning walk experience into a formal feedback system. A word of caution is critical at this point. Keeping the formal evaluation system apart from this process avoids any misunderstandings and loss of trust on the part of the participants. In other words, if teachers begin to see what happened on the Collegial Learning Walks in their formal evaluations, the intention of the process has been violated, and the administrator will lose the teachers' trust.

After participating in a Collegial Learning Walk with Leslie Collings, Dave Morris, Associate Superintendent of Learning in Rocky View School Division, Alberta, Canada, had the following comments:

"I can see how this process can be valuable with teachers within and across departments. It offers the capacity to build and generate ideas quickly that would take a long time if you tried to develop them in isolation. I liked the ideas the group can generate with the last question that focuses on "kick it up a notch." It is not overwhelming.

If the CLW's focus is on the teacher, the teacher being observed is under stress. But if the purpose is for the group to learn, the stress is not there. The process is truly generative. For example, the debriefing question about authentic learning is valuable because it drills down to the common understandings of the group. It must be non-judgmental and non-evaluative. If it goes down that avenue (evaluation), it will not work. Administrators (like most teachers) naturally want to fix. They want to tell and

HOW IS THE PROCESS A CONTINUOUS GROWTH MODEL?

correct. Instead, with this process, common definitions can emerge that make sense to the entire group. The CLW is a vehicle to demonstrate what ideas really mean and how they evolve into increased student learning."

CHAPTER 9

How does the process build a learning community?

Tell me and I'll forget. Show me, and I may not remember. Involve me, and I'll understand.
—Native American Saying

Where a spirit of collaboration already exists in the building, the networking and collaboration will just grow in geometric proportions. If a true climate of collaboration is non-existent, then the Collegial Learning Walks will spark ideas to begin the collaboration internally. As this spark begins, the principal needs to fan that spark by providing time for collaboration during the school day, perhaps even facilitate it initially.

Lynn Brewer and Tammy Wolverton, East Central Upper Elementary administrators, have taken part in The University of Southern Mississippi Gulf Coast Leadership Center for the past three years. "Through this professional development, we have gained a world of knowledge and resources to help us manage our learning environment more effectively," says Lynn Brewer. She continues,

"One of the most beneficial concepts we have learned is the Collegial Learning Walks. The team-based structure of a CLW encourages collaborative conversations among participants about the nature of teaching and learning, which can lead to decisions and actions that are deeply rooted in the classroom experience.

It was important for us to set the stage for this new experience by articulating to the staff our focus and purpose of these visits. A conversation took place in grade level meetings that led teachers to think about student learning and engagement. As we brought teachers to an understanding that we are all learners helping each other improve our own skills, it became evident that teachers are intimidated by peers and administrators "watching" them. As administrators, we tried the Collegial Learning Walks to demonstrate to teachers how these walks would be conducted. This presented a a two-fold benefit: it helped teachers to understand the process, and it gave administrators an opportunity to practice the skills prior to using a team. As we talked to students in classrooms and discussed the student learning and engagement we were observing, teachers became comfortable with the process.

Recently, I took the curriculum team to one of our ILC (Instructional Leadership Center) conversations, and they were able to participate in a Collegial Learning Walk. The comments from my team were very positive, and they enjoyed being able to practice this new concept in a school that was not their home school. Our next step is to divide the campus into teams, allowing every teacher to be on a team. One day per week a different team will go with the administration as we conduct our Collegial Learning Walks.

I see this process as an ongoing professional development for the entire staff as they take things away from the walks to use in their rooms and as they receive feedback from the walk about how they could step it up. This is a "win win" for everyone. A nice way to build on what is working is to examine student work collaboratively following a protocol that focuses the activity and prevents it from becoming a controversial experience. What a learning experience CLWs are for everyone involved!

CHAPTER 10

What is the "magic" of the process? How does it work best?

I am still learning.
—Michelangelo

Simply stated, the magic is the co-construction of meaning in a community of trust and support. It is not just one "silver bullet" but a process. The classroom conversations with the students are essential to be able to have the meaningful dialogue that follows. Everyone on the walk needs to feel safe and needs to be heard totally devoid of judgment. The questions addressed in the protocol, by design, aim to produce rich dialogue that is not mechanical and merely surface level. Because everyone has a "common" synchronous experience, the creation of meaning that follows is layered and robust. We say "common" because although we all walk into the same classroom, our experience will be our own experience resulting from our own frame of reference and prior knowledge. The task during the walk is to make connections of our common understandings and build on what each one brings to the table. Once everyone feels heard and a contributing member of this meaning-making bank of ideas and understandings, the process begins to flow with one idea building on the last. It is critical that the Collegial Learning Walk's leader include everyone in the discussions, paraphrasing and summarizing to begin embroidering those

A VALUE ADDED DECISION

common understandings. A tacit agreement is that, by virtue of being on the walk, every person must contribute to the group thinking. Since all the questions evoke a particular key component, all must be asked, immediately followed by a brief reflection to capture the essence of the discussion. The entire experience must be debriefed after all individual classroom visits have also been properly debriefed. An insight-producing question is *what was your experience of the Collegial Learning Walk? What did you take away from the entire experience?* Having that discussion with the small group of Collegial Learning Walk members validates their insights and questions. It is not surprising if the group generates more questions that will take the experience to yet a different level of meaning-making and transfer.

Below are excerpts from teachers who have participated on Collegial Learning Walks:

Mary Robbins: "Seems to me, Learning Walks might 'show' kids the importance of their lessons and practice, because the teachers visit with real interest about their insights. This was a really cool experience."

Megan Cravens: "To piggy back on what others were saying, it was really neat to just walk into other classrooms to see what strategies were implemented and how their classroom became a community! Thanks again for letting us come in."

Carrie Shaughnessy: "The learning walks are valuable in seeing how kids are engaged and if transfer is present........ all the other things we walked away with are a bonus!"

Casey Otemuyiwa: "I came away with several ideas

that I can (and will) use at some point in my own classroom. I think the list of questions to ask students that were printed on the 'Preparation for Learning Walks' document are great ones for getting to the heart of what's really important."

After six years of on-going implementation, **Jennifer Westcott** at Monteleone Junior High School in Louisiana asserts, "Teachers are more comfortable with learning walks because they support growth and do not focus on failure. The learning walks allow us to gather real time data to positively impact student learning, have reflective conversations, discuss best practices, and most importantly, improve student achievement."

Participating administrators from around the country have had similar reactions.

Laurie Pitre, principal of one of Mississippi's Blue Ribbon elementary schools and a member of The University of Southern Mississippi Instructional Leadersip Center, said, "I think the questions that we are asking and the answers that are generated have the potential for tremendous teacher growth and ultimately student achievement. It is also so much more effective to "debrief" with others, to hear their insights and observations rather than going it alone."

Sandra Garbowicz, Director of Teaching and Learning in Beaver Dam Unified School District in Wisconsin, says that the adult collaboration chatter is powerful because the student's voice is included. "You are not speculating, and nothing is staged. It's about the adults making meaning leading to transfer and the domino effect that it will have in the classroom."

A VALUE ADDED DECISION

Preliminary Quantitative Data Gathering

One school where the Collegial Learning Walks have been central to the school's continuous improvement is Monteleone Junior High School in St. Tammany Parish, Louisiana. For the 2010-11 School Year 34% of the school population qualified for free and reduced lunch. Since its inception in August, 2005, the same year Hurricane Katrina devastated the area, the school has met its growth target and made 'Adequate Yearly Progress' every year.

When asked to what she attributed the continued and steady success of the school, the principal, Donna Addison, said, "I attribute it to our collaborative environment, and the Collegial Learning Walks have been a major avenue for collaboration. When you have a collaborative environment and the guaranteed curriculum, which is actually a collaborative living document, you have a winning situation. Our teachers helped write our guaranteed curriculum, and they continue to collaborate as it evolves and gets better every day. The learning walks support its implementation and put our teachers in meaningful and supportive collegial conversations on a regular basis. The product that this environment generated is the yearly improvement in our school's test scores."

Table 1:
LP Monteleone Junior High School School Performance Scores Determined by the Louisiana Accountability System.

School Year	2006-07	2007-08	2008-09	2009-10
School Performance score	101.5	103.4	111.3	112.7

WHAT IS THE "MAGIC" OF THE PROCESS?

Note:

School Performance Scores are calculated using schools' index scores, multiplied by their corresponding weight.

All Growth School Performance Score (SPS) calculations are based on one year of data.

All Baseline SPS calculations are based on two years of data, including test data from the two most recent spring administrations and attendance, dropout and/or graduation data from two and three years prior.

Source: Louisiana Department of Education Website: http://www.doe.state.la.us/data/school_accountability_reports.aspx

Kim Brandon, Principal at Parkway Northeast Middle School, who this year implemented Collegial Learning Walks with all teachers, conducted a survey of all her teachers relative to what they learned from the Collegial Learning Walks. Following are a few of the comments she received from the respondents:

1. "The Collegial Learning Walks have reminded me of the importance of keeping purpose and transfer front and center. I am not where I want it to be yet. I am still working on taking children through making meaning to get them to transfer."

2. "It was helpful to see student engagement in other subject areas and to think about how that could be applied to my classroom."

3. "Engagement can look different in different classrooms and be different for every student."

4. "I have made a conscious attempt to monitor the level of engagement during my lessons and collaborate with teachers in order to find ways to increase engagement by gradually releasing responsibility."

5. "I think about engagement a lot more than I did before the learning walks. We (I) prep for a lesson and pull out my plans—I look them over and think about how I can make sure there is more engagement and deeper levels of learning for students so they will remember what they learn."

6. "The learning walks gave me some perspective and plenty of ideas to implement what I once knew as good instruction, but I had lost sight of them with all of the skill and drill previously required by standardized testing."

CHAPTER 11
What are the "do nots" to be avoided at all cost?

Success is more permanent when you achieve it without destroying your principles.
—Walter Cronkite

Following are words of caution about practices that could sabotage your efforts:

Do not force anyone to go on a Collegial Learning Walk or to be the teacher the group goes to visit.

Do not judge any component, and steer the group away from judgment.

Do not impose your thinking. Allow the group to co-create their own meaning.

Do not link the process to evaluation. From the beginning, make it very clear that this is a professional development, job-embedded process that is not in any way part of personnel evaluation.

Do not hurry it along. Be patient. Honor everyone's think time and processing.

Do not deviate from the protocol. Make sure that the experience you debrief includes a conversation with the students and that you debrief the experience immediately after the visit. Include a minimum of 3-4 classroom visits during one Collegial Learning Walk cycle.

Do not delegate your role as leader to anyone other than another building administrator who "gets it" and who evaluates teachers.

Do not discuss what happened on a learning walk. Get permission to use the experience as an example.

Donna Addison is principal of Monteleone Junior High in St. Tammany Parish in Louisiana. A veteran of the process, she describes her own experience: "We have been doing Collegial Learning Walks for several years. When we first started, it was scary. As we presented it to our teachers, we did it in a very professional manner, telling them we would visit classrooms and learn from each other. We would debrief in the hall and always started with what we would take away. That gave the teachers a positive outlook. They knew we would be looking for good things that we would be able to take back to our classrooms. They knew we were not looking to cut them down or see what was wrong with their teaching.

"As we grew the CLWs, we were able to have deeper conversations, talking about the purpose of the lesson, the engagement, the transfer and so forth. What we know is that the only way to answer those questions is to talk to the students. It's to the point now that when we walk in, the students are telling us, 'We are working on this today,

WHAT ARE THE "DO NOTS"?

and this is what we are learning.' We can see that they are challenged beyond surface understanding. At the beginning, we just talked about pretty bulletin boards. Now, that is not even a part of the discussion. We are talking about the real challenges. Students are able to tell us about their learning."

Her advice to her colleagues: "It is a scary thing, and my friends tell me about their fears. First, remember to start small, start with the positive and grow the process because it is so worth it. It has been a learning process for me as well. I have coached teachers to improve their crafts and have, therefore, professionally grown myself."

One key element to remember is that the fear of evaluation will be one to overcome and not necessarily evaluation by administration. Peer evaluation and criticism is another source of fear. Mary Yarborough, a teacher at the same school, reflects on her six years of experience with her principal, Donna Addison, conducting learning walks. She comments, "I think teachers need to see what is going on in other classrooms, and not be secluded in their own rooms. I feel I have become a better teacher since we started learning walks at our school. Teachers have to be led into this process correctly through strong leadership, because it can be scary to put yourself out there and allow colleagues to come in and see what you're doing."

Cassidy Kemp, an ESL teacher at the Sullivan's School in Japan, echoes the same concern and offers a viable suggestion, "CLWs could not simply be implemented school wide. It would be better to begin implementing them with a group of teachers supportive of the idea in order to make them best fit the school culture and to work out any minor problems. It could be piloted with volunteer teachers willing to do the

A VALUE ADDED DECISION

CLWs and have others observe in their classrooms."

Gauging the climate of the school will be a significant first step to determine what will be first steps toward the change in focus from looking at what the teacher is doing to studying what the students are doing with the work provided to them. It will be essential to build the level of trust among the faculty that assures them of the real intention of the process. **Remember that we have wisdom in our buildings. We just have to use it.** We know what to do. We know when our students are not making meaning and transferring what they have learned. We just need to bring what we do know into our level of awareness so that we can analyze it, talk about it and just do it! Without exception, principals ready to engage in meaningful dialogue about instruction exude a tremendous amount of enthusiasm for the process. From April Nobles in Bogalusa City Schools, Bogalusa, Louisiana, we received this message following the first learning walk experience she facilitated, "It was 'AWE'some! I was on Cloud nine yesterday. The first two groups I took were incredible. They walked away with a good understanding that they need to relinquish control to the students. They are seeing that in order for students to transfer their learning, the students must be 'doing.' That was the greatest thing to come out of our walks. It was an extremely positive experience and led to great discussions. I am excited and energized!"

CHAPTER 12

Conclusion

We have all the answers inside just waiting for us to discover them.
—Gignoux

A great deal of thinking about educational change as it relates to student achievement and engagement is framed in terms of preparing students for their future in either securing gainful employment or attending institutions of higher learning. The Collegial Learning Walks, which have proven successful through six years of research, create an opportunity for teachers and administrators to create conversations that will improve teaching and learning for entire educational communities.

Yes, in the past we have blamed everyone and everything for the shortcomings in education. Now, however, it is time to put that in the past and realize we do have the tool we need to increase student achievement by ensuring that every student has the opportunity to acquire knowledge, make meaning of it, and then transfer what is learned to new and/or unique situations and with deeper depths of understanding. Teachers and educational leaders have the greatest impact on students' learning. One teacher summed it all up when she said, "As a result of what I have learned on a Collegial Learning Walk, I now know that I, too, must be engaged in learning all the time. I prepare for my students but it's also about my learning.

It's the best form of modeling I can provide and the way to keep my saw sharpened all the time." Isn't it time we work together to make a difference for every child in every classroom?

APPENDIX A

Collegial Learning Walks Summary

Collegial Learning Walks Summary

What it is	What it is not
• It is a process designed to look for what's next in our learning about learning.	• It is not a process designed to find what is wrong.
• It is a collaborative, generative professional development process designed to support everyone's thinking about instructional practice.	• There are no presuppositions that anyone is broken or defective in their practice.
• It is designed to raise questions and promote self-reflection.	• It is not putting anyone on notice of improvement.
• It is a process that will eventually promote a way of being in an instructional community, of sharing, of coaching, of examining practice with no particular agenda in mind.	• It is not designed for the implementation of any particular improvement strategy.

• It requires an administrator willing to be vulnerable and open to learning each day.	• It is not designed to put anyone's practice under scrutiny, critique, or improvement.
• It is a program of attraction since no one is forced to participate.	• It is not a static group or network.
• It is open to possibilities yet firm in its supportive commitment.	• It is not designed to have a focus on a common "problem or practice."

Important: **The process is designed for the learning of the people on the walk**

Recommendations:

1. The principal leads the process.

2. Withhold ALL judgment.

3. Observe in classrooms where everyone is able to talk to the students.

Agreements of the Collegial Learning Walks

1. We are all learners helping each other improve our own skills.

2. No one is "there" yet.

3. We are not here to judge.

4. We are not looking for anything in particular, just "effective" instruction leading to transfer.

5. We record nothing.

6. We refrain from talking to the teacher.

7. We maintain strict confidentiality.

8. We agree that the only thing over which we have control is the quality of the work we provide our students.

The Release of Responsibility

1. I do; you watch.

2. I do; you help.

3. You do; I help.

4. You do; I watch.

The process moves into the classroom:

Walk in the classroom for a few minutes.

If possible, talk to the students and ask questions. Look around the room for artifacts and evidence of authenticity and challenge.

In the classroom, we ask the students the following or similar questions:

1. What are you learning?

2. What are you being asked to do?

3. How is this like something you have already learned?

4. What will you do with this?

5. What will it help you do?

6. Why is it important to know this?

Immediately after, we step outside for the debriefing led by the principal.

Debriefing Questions

1. What did you observe that you could take away immediately?

2. What was the teacher enabling the students to do? (What was the point of the task students were asked to do?)

3. Was the teacher taking the students to transfer? How do you know?

4. Were the students engaged in making meaning? Did you observe evidence of understanding?

5. What percent of the students were engaged in making meaning leading to transfer? How do you know? How many were compliant? How do you know?

6. What was it about the work that made it engaging/authentic?

7. Did you see evidence of authentic learning?

8. How was the release of responsibility?

9. What could the teacher have done to "kick it up a notch?

Follow-up questions after the *FIRST* collegial learning walk:

1. What are your "take-aways" from the entire experience? (Make sure everyone offers something.)

2. What effect did the group conversation have for you? (Go around to capture everyone's personal experience with the mediated conversation.)

3. What's next for you?

4. What could we have done to "kick it up a notch?'

The Power is in the Mediated Conversation.

APPENDIX B
Practitioners cited in the text

Donna Addison
Principal
Monteleone Junior High School
St. Tammany Parish Schools
Louisiana

Lynn Brewer
Principal
East Central Upper Elementary
Jackson County Schools
Mississippi

Megan Cravens
Teacher
Northeast Middle School
Parkway School District
Missouri

Kim Brandon
Principal
Northeast Middle School
Parkway School District
Missouri

Leslie Collings
Principal
Springbank Community High School
Rocky View School Division
Alberta, Canada

Tally Drawdy
5th Grade Teacher
East Central Upper Elementary
Jackson County Schools
Mississippi

Sandy Garbowicz
Director of Teaching and
  Learning
Beaver Dam School
  District
Wisconsin

Amanda Knight
4th Grade Teacher
East Central Upper
  Elementary
Jackson County Schools
Mississippi

Deborah McCollum
Principal
Covington High School
St. Tammany Parish
  School District
Louisiana

Aaron Nisbett
Teacher
Springbank Community
  High School
Rocky View School
  Division
Alberta, Canada

Cassidy Kemp
ESL Teacher
The Sullivan's School
Yokosuka, Kanagawa
Japan

Chad Knowler
Teacher
Springbank Community
  High School
Rocky View School
  Division
Alberta, Canada

Dave Morris
Associate Superintendent
  of Learning
Rocky View School
  Division
Alberta, Canada

Casey Otemuyiwa
Teacher
Northeast Middle School
Parkway School District
Missouri

PRACTITIONERS CITED IN THE TEXT

Carol Pearsons
Teacher
East Central Upper
  Elementary
Jackson County Schools,
  Mississippi

Lauri Pitre
Principal
Northbay Elementary
Biloxi Public Schools
Mississippi

Jessica Reynolds
Teacher
Springbank Community
  High School
Rocky View School
  Division
Alberta, Canada

Mary Robbins
Teacher
Northeast Middle School
Parkway School District
Missouri

Tara Rostad
Teacher
Springbank Community
  High School
Rocky View School
  Division
Alberta, Canada

Carrie Shaughnessy
Teacher
Northeast Middle School
Parkway School District
Missouri

Jennifer Westcott
Teacher
Monteleone Junior High
  School
St. Tammany Parish
  Schools
Louisiana

Mary Yarborough
Teacher
Monteleone Junior High
  School
St. Tammany Parish
  Schools
Louisiana

References

City, Elmore, Fiarman &Teitel. (2009). Instructional rounds in education. Cambridge, MA: Harvard Education Press.

Costa and Garmston (2002). Cognitive coaching: a foundation for Renaissance schools.

Fullan, Michael. Quoted in *Unmistakable Impact* by Jim Knight.

Guilott, M & Parker, G (2010, Summer). Reconciling IDEIA and NCLB in St. Tammany Parish. Educational Horizons, 86(4), 231-248.

Marzano, Robert. (2003), What Works in Schools. Alexandria, VA: Association for Supervision and Curriculum Development.

Miller, G. A. (1956). The magical number seven, plus or minus two: some limits on our capacity for processing information. *Psychological Review.* 63 (2): 343-355.

National Research Council (2000): How people learn: brain, mind, experience and school. Washington, D.C.: National Academy Press

Schlecty, Phillip (2009). *Profile elements.* Retrieved from the worldwide web.

Schmoker, Mike. (2006). Results Now. Alexandria, VA: Association for Supervision and Curriculum Development, pp. 9-46.

Wiggins, G & McTighe, J. (2005). Understanding by Design. Alexandria, VA: Association for Supervision and Curriculum Development.

Wiggins, G & McTighe, J. (2007). Schooling by Design. Alexandria, VA: Association for Supervision and Curriculum Development.

Wiggins, G & McTighe, J. (May 2008). Put understanding first. Educational Leadership, 65(8), 36-41.

Wood Ray, Katie (2006). What are you thinking? Educational Leadership. ASCD

CPSIA information can be obtained at www.ICGtesting.com
Printed in the USA
BVOW03s1643151014

370964BV00013B/265/P

9 781432 785765